DEDICATION

This book is dedicated to all of those talented, unsung, so-called
amateur songwriters – in song-circles and coffee-houses and
open-mics, in living-rooms, and front-porches, sitting around
campfires or in messy college dorms, all over the world - whose
inspired works may never blast out of a car radio or provide
background music for an elevator ride or visit to the mall (though
some, no doubt, will), but whose passion, earnestness, dedication,
raw talent and skill, weave notes and lyrics together into personal,
idiosyncratic, miraculous works of transcendent beauty and joy.
Those are the best songs of all.

DEAN FRIEDMAN

THE SONGWRITER'S HANDBOOK

CONTENTS

DEAN FRIEDMAN

DISCLAIMER

Just to be clear, this handbook offers my very personal take on how to write a song. But the reality is every songwriter has a unique and individual style, their own way of looking at the world, and their own approach to crafting a song. Which is, in my view, exactly as it should be. I believe a song ought to be a personal expression, possessed of a unique and individual voice. Those are always my favorite kinds of songs. And though my writing is often described as eclectic, I don't profess to know how to write *all* kinds of songs. But, for what it's worth, I *do* know how to write a pretty decent Dean Friedman song.

I say that for this reason: many of the examples in this handbook will be drawn from my own songs as I attempt to relay my recollection of how they were written. I definitely plan to offer up plenty of examples by other songwriters, but I can only guess at what they may have had in mind, when they wrote a particular lyric or musical phrase. When I offer up an example of my own writing it's because, in most cases, I have a pretty vivid recollection of what I was thinking at the time and how I approached a particular writing challenge… and that just might provide you with some insight into an otherwise vague and nebulous process.

As I said a moment ago, it's my strongly held opinion that your song ought to express *your* point of view and speak with *your* unique voice - the more idiosyncratic the better, as far as I'm concerned. My goal here is not to teach you how to write a generic, derivative pop song that sounds like every other song on the radio. My goal is to provide you with some useful tools that can help you to express yourself using words and music, to write songs that mean something to you and, if you're lucky, mean something to the people that hear them.

DEAN FRIEDMAN

INTRODUCTION

This is going to be a skinny book.

That's because I believe the essence of songwriting can be described in a handful of chapters; and certainly in a book slim enough to shove into your back pocket. Also, I've purposely left out some of the standard content typically included in songwriting books, such as chapters on how to copyright your songs, how to demo your songs, how to sell your songs, and how to negotiate song contracts. That information is easy to find, in a zillion places, if you are interested in finding it. Some of it's actually useful. Those are not the concerns of this book.

As far as I'm concerned, *it's the creation of the song itself, that's important.*

If it pleases you, if it moves you, if it cracks you up, if it fills you with delight or sends a chill up your spine, if the act of writing it provides a cathartic emotional release, or just plain tickles the hell out of you… those things matter. And if somebody else likes it, too. Well, hey, that's even better. But not necessary, in my book.

My book is about the art and craft of writing songs. They don't have to be hits, though I've written my share. Some of the songs I'm most proud of have never been played on the radio. They don't even have to be ear-catchingly popular. But they should be yours, a product of your own self-expression, the result of your earnest efforts. As such, they have real inherent value – and even if everyone else, and their mother, thinks they suck!... so what?

INSPIRATION vs CRAFT

Anybody can write a song.

You don't have to be a trained musician and you don't have to be an English lit major. The Beatles could barely read music and 'Happy Birthday', one of the most popular songs of all time, was written by Patty Hill, a kindergarten teacher from Kentucky, and her sister, Mildred, back in 1893 (incredibly, Warner/Chappell Music is still collecting royalties on it.)

All you need is a love of songs and a burning desire – or insistent curiosity - to create one of your own. After that, the hardest part is just sitting still, in one place, long enough for your song to come bursting out of you. Well, sometimes, instead of bursting out, they bubble out, and sometimes you have to drag them out kicking and screaming. But they're in there – in all of us – just waiting to be born, if you just give them half a chance.

Here's a confession: I don't really know *exactly* how I write my own songs.

Huh? Now, don't go running to get your money back, just yet. Sure, I've had chart-topping hits around the world, and been critically acclaimed (though the editor of NME once wrote that my singing sounded like Kermit the Frog on Quaaludes ;-). I've earned my share of gold records, shipped millions of units... but the truth is, I don't really know *where* those hit-making lyrics, melodic hooks and infectious phrases came from. Most writers, if they're honest, will make a similar admission. Sure, I'll take credit for them (and collect the royalties, thank you very much), but the initial inspiration is still inexplicable to me. What's not inexplicable is the *craft* of songwriting. That's what happens before and after inspiration hits. The craft of songwriting is a collection of techniques and choices that any songwriter can employ to, first, invite inspiration and, then, to channel and shape it, once it arrives.

That word *choice* is important. In fact, it's mostly what this book is about – the choices you can make will determine where your song goes, how it evolves, and what it turns into. Basically, I view the craft of songwriting as a series of **questions** that you, the songwriter, asks about your song; the **answers** to those questions lead you to make certain **choices**, and those choices ultimately shape your song.

As I've already confessed, I can't teach you to be inspired. (Relax... with a little coaxing, it'll come.) However, I can offer some practical suggestions for how to *invite* inspiration to strike. Think, Ben Franklin's experiments with electricity: It's not easy catching lighting in a bottle, but if you stand outside in the middle of a lighting storm, flying a kite with a metal key tied to its tail, you'll greatly increase the odds. So it is with inspiration. Like catching lighting in a bottle, it just requires a plan and a bit of patience and persistence. Eventually, it will come. (and, usually, with minimal risk of electrocution)

Here's what I do know, here's what I can teach you, and here's what this book is about:

1. INSPIRATION: I can offer suggestions for how to create an optimum environment for inspiration to strike along with a few helpful tricks for teasing it out of you.

...and

2. CRAFT: I can offer suggestions for how to channel that inspiration when it, arrives, suddenly – out of the blue – and hits you over the head ('splatt') like a rubber mallet in a Tom & Jerry cartoon.

This book will start off with a brief discussion of inspiration and then the rest of the book will deal mostly with craft. But understand that in some ways that distinction between inspiration and craft is arbitrary, even irrelevant. In reality, inspiration is a part of every single choice you make while exercising that craft. And there are some professional songwriters who are completely dismissive of the whole idea of inspiration. The great Cole Porter is quoted as saying, *"My sole inspiration is a telephone call from a director."* There's a lot to be said for this practical point of view.

But it could be we're quibbling over semantics here. For our immediate purposes, let's stick with the concept that inspiration is what generates creative ideas and craft is how you shape them into a song.

For readers that like to skip ahead, here's a super-condensed outline of how this book approaches the process of writing a song:

1. **Improvise** - to invite inspiration.
2. **Ask questions** - understanding what you've already done will provide you clues about what to do next.
3. **Figure out what your song is about** – the sooner, the better. Once you know what your song is about, you'll have a goal, and a clearer path, and strategy, for reaching your destination.
4. **Make choices** – exercise some control over how your song takes shape by understanding how different choices can lead you in different directions.
5. **Write a whole lot of lines and couplets** – fill a page or more with ideas, phrases and couplets that pertain to your main theme. Overwrite to get yourself in the creative flow and to give yourself lots of material to choose from.
6. **Whittle it down** (edit) – pick the best stuff, as long as it serves the overall goal of the composition, and shape it into a finished song.

There's a bit more to it than that, but the above should give you some idea of what's in store. Keep in mind that there are as many different approaches to writing a song as there are songwriters – this is just one. And to be honest, this isn't even an approach I use myself, on every occasion. In fact, every time I sit down to write a song, it's a totally new experience. That's part of the fun… and what also makes it little scary. But like any experienced songwriter, who's written more than a few hundred songs, you start to notice certain patterns; you discover devices and techniques that can help you out of a jam. This book is my attempt to describe some of those recognizable patterns and to articulate some of the familiar steps I take, and conscious choices I find myself making, over and over again, while I'm writing a song.

You actually know most of this stuff intuitively anyway, simply by virtue of having listened to music for most of your life. My goal here is to awaken that innate knowledge, and add to it with some specific suggestions about how you can best put it to use when writing your own songs.

One more thing, before I continue: Throughout this handbook, I'll be urging the reader (you) to go online and listen to the various songs I point to as examples of different aspects of songwriting. It is highly recommended that you actually listen to all these songs, in order for you to get the full impact of this book. I've created an online 'playlist' with links to every song title mentioned in this handbook. As you're reading, take the time to click through and hear for yourself what I'm talking about.

Here's the online 'Playlist' page:

www.deanfriedman.com/songwriters-handbook-playlist.html

NOTE: eBook and online editions of this book, may also contain links embedded in the Song Titles themselves, but you may find the above 'Playlist' page just as useful.

Any questions?

Good. I'll try to answer them as best I can.

Here goes…

INSPIRATION

Inspiration is the most crucial ingredient in songwriting – that mysterious creative spark that spawns an idea, a musical line or a lyrical phrase.

But before I talk about techniques for inviting inspiration over for a visit, I should probably state the obvious - but not always easy to accomplish - which is: find yourself a quiet place where you can, hopefully, work with minimal or, preferably, *no* distractions, and carve out enough time for yourself to dedicate to the task at hand.

Easier said than done, I know. As a father that works out of a home-studio, which was frequently visited by rambunctious kids (now grown), I fully appreciate the challenge required to find uninterrupted time and space in which to create. You do the best you can. And as a last resort, remember, there's a reason musicians keep *'musician hours'*.

Of course, inspiration can strike at any time and in any place, so it's also a good idea to keep a pen and notepad or smartphone handy to record your ideas.

O.K., so you've run all your errands, the house is empty, the phone's on mute, you're ready to create…

Here are four techniques for getting inspired (there are plenty more you can probably think of yourself, but these should get you started): 1. Listen, 2. Improvise, 3. Following Your Nose, 4. Stand on Your Head.

Let's start with,

#1: Listen.

Listen to songs. That's all there is to it.

Yes, I know this sounds pretty obvious – because it is. But it's also true and worth thinking seriously about. Other songwriters are our first and most powerful inspiration.

Because that's really how songwriters are made – from Stephen Foster to Irving Berlin to Carole King to Lennon & McCartney to Stevie Wonder to Laura Nyro to Regina Spektor; they grew up absorbing the songs of their childhood and teens and the minute they learned a few chords, they started writing their own songs. I'm not talking about plagiarism here. I'm referring to the positive way in which all artists are influenced by the artists that went before them as well as by their peers. The trick is to absorb all those influences and then transform them into something original and uniquely your own.

So, don't be shy.

Listen to what other songwriters have done. Turn on your radio, pop in a CD, download an mp3 (legal or otherwise), call a friend and go listen to live music at a local club (support live music! Musicians gotta eat - especially after you've just illegally downloaded all their mp3's for free! ;-). Listen and learn. Fill your ears with songs. Soak 'em up, absorb them, assimilate them, enjoy them, get passionate about them. And allow yourself to be influenced by them. It's O.K.!

> *"For a songwriter, you don't really go to songwriting school; you learn by listening to tunes. And you try to understand them and take them apart and see what they're made of, and wonder if you can make one, too."*
> Tom Waits

When I first started writing songs, at the age of 9 (A cheerful little four-chord, ditty entitled, 'I'd Love To Take A Swim With You in the Summer Time'), it was not a conscious act. Technique and craft were not part of the process. I was like a little monkey, simply imitating my elders, (including, among others, the Monkees!) This is a form of benign plagiarism. All writers practice it, starting out. It's the process by which music is passed from generation to generation, from artist to artist. Dylan imitated Woody Guthrie and Hank Williams. Lennon and McCartney imitated Goffin and King. These were their crucial influences. Every songwriter is the product of the continuum of music that went before them and that continues to circulate all around them. Then, somewhere along the line, the fledgling writer finds their own voice and steps out from under the influence of their musical mentors, to create something unique and original – something of their own. Something that may well influence the next generation of songwriters.

Don't skip this fundamental step. Yes, it's obvious and yes, you've been doing it all your life, but it's worth repeating. Expose yourself to great songwriters – you be the judge, there are plenty out there (and plenty referenced in this book). Absorb what they have to offer.

Listening to those songs, learning those songs, playing those songs… that's how you lay the groundwork, that's where a songwriter *really* learns how to write. And it's that fertile ground from which inspiration will eventually germinate and sprout (although, admittedly, if I'd been a bit more choosier with my influences I might've come up with a slightly snappier metaphor, just then.)

> NOTE: Borrowing an idea and drastically transforming it to suit your needs is fine – great artists do it all the time. Listen to John Lennon's, 'Norwegian Wood', and Dylan's, 'Fourth Time Around', back to back, both waltzes in ¾ time, and see if you can guess just who influenced who?*
>
> *Email me for the answer: dean@deanfriedman.com

Immerse yourself in the songs of artists you admire and then try composing your own versions in a similar style. Don't be shy or self-conscious. It's O.K. to borrow. We all do it. You have permission to be derivative, and imitative in your early efforts. In doing so, you will be absorbing invaluable lessons in form, structure and style. That knowledge will become innate. And inevitably, filtered through your own unique experiences and personality, those lessons will evolve into a style of your own.

Of course, it does pay to choose your influences carefully!

I began writing the opening track of my first album while still in college after having purchased a beautiful sounding Martin D35 acoustic guitar, paid for with my first student loan (meant to pay for books, but the guitar turned out to be a better long-term investment). I had just learned the fingerpicking guitar part to Paul McCartney's classic, 'Blackbird', and perversely thought, "what would happen if I played that lovely fingerpicking progression backwards?". This eventually turned into the song, 'Company', co-written by the extremely talented singer-songwriter, Stuffy Shmitt. The point is, instead of 'Company', I might have titled the song, 'Dribkcalb', because essentially, with some critical variations, it's 'Blackbird' played backwards. I relayed this anecdote during a masterclass I gave at the Liverpool Institute for Performing Arts [L.I.P.A.], a music and art university founded by Paul McCartney. Afterwards, an instructor informed me that during his occasional visits, Paul would relay to L.I.P.A. students that when he wrote his song, 'Blackbird', it was heavily influenced by a classical guitar piece he'd learned as a kid – J.S. Bach's Bourrée in E minor.

Which just goes to prove my earlier point, *choose your influences carefully!*

McCartney also has a saying he shares with L.I.P.A. students which acknowledges the fundamental value of absorbing the influences of other musicians while avoiding overt plagiarism, and that is: 'Steal with humility'.

I would simply expand on that sage advice by adding, Steal with humility – and *stealth!*

> *"My songwriting and my style became more complex as I listened, learned, borrowed and stole and put my music together.* - Boz Scaggs

10

So, *listen!* And don't just limit yourself to songs, by the way. Listen to all kinds of music, poetry, drama. Listen to the traffic. Listen to your neighbors arguing. Listen to the news. Listen to the weather report. Listen to the guy at the corner news stand. You'll find inspiration all around you – you just have to learn when to recognize it.

O.K. I've listened to all these inspiring songwriters, but I'm still stuck. Now, what do I do?

#2: Improvise

Sometimes a song idea will arrive unbidden and unexpected. When that happens, be sure to say thank you to your muse. (They can be fickle, so best not to piss them off.) But you don't always want to just sit around waiting for inspiration to strike. Sometimes you want to invite it in. Entice it. Set the stage. Make it feel right at home. Improvisation – noodling, riffing, fiddling around - is one of the best ways to do that.

Pick up an instrument, sit down at a piano, a music sequencer, a word processor … and just *play* (in every sense of the word). Get those fingers moving. Make some noise. Play some chords. String some words together. If it sounds like nonsense, that's good! It should sound ridiculous at first. You're still priming the pump, opening up the spigot to let the ideas begin to flow. Give 'em a chance. You need to unclog the pipes at the beginning.

Don't worry about how stupid everything may sound when you're just starting out. Be patient. Relax. Don't stop. Just keep playing.

Whether you're improvising with notes or words, the basic approach is the same – you want to *play*, you want to have *fun*, *experiment* and *explore*. It's sort of like musical finger-painting. Dip your fingers into the notes and words and swirl them around.

If you're taking a 'music first' approach, experiment with different chord progressions, try new voicings and fingerings, play around with different melodic patterns and phrases. If you're taking a 'lyric first' approach, free associate with nonsense words and phrases. Put down anything that pops into your head no matter how absurd. Be child-like. Be stupid. Have fun!

> NOTE: Every songwriter since biblical times, when David was busy seducing young maidens under the olive trees, with his golden voice and lute (this was in his post-Goliath, pre-King days), has been prompted to answer the age old interview question, 'Which comes first, the words or the music?'. For the benefit of radio DJ's everywhere, I shall now provide the unequivocal answer to this, frankly, annoying question. The answer is...
>
> It depends.
>
> That's it. That's the answer! Every song is different. And every songwriter, or pair of collaborating songwriters, is different. The process is different every single time. Sometimes they even arrive together like a pair of uncoordinated puppies climbing over each other to squeeze through the door and play outside.
>
> This is like asking 'Which do you spread first, the peanut butter or the jelly?' (The peanut butter, of course.)
>
> I hope that finally sets the matter to rest, once and for all. (not very likely)

If you don't know where to start, just open up your mouth and start singing - anything. Scat-sing. Doobie doo wah, biddy bop, la, la, la... Sing on nonsense words. Use *place-setters*; those are random words that you sing over a melody until you decide on the actual lyrics. EXAMPLE: the most famous instance of a lyric place-setter would be Paul McCartney singing, *'Scrambled Eggs'*, in place of the lyric, *'Yesterday'*, before he finally came up with the actual lyrics. [NOTE: *'Scrambled Eggs'* has the same number of syllables as *'Yesterday'*.]

If your improvisations still sound dumb after 5 minutes. Don't quit yet! Take a breath… and *keep going!*

The writer Dorothy Parker once famously said, *'writing is the act of placing one's behind in a chair.'* There's not much more to it than that. There are no guarantees that you'll come up with something useable every time, but the odds are pretty good that if you keep going, sure enough, after a while, you'll happen upon a fresh idea - an intriguing musical phrase, an interesting chord progression, a curious lyric - and that's all you need to start a song.

It doesn't have to be much. It could be the tiniest kernel of an idea - two chords, a few words strung together, a guitar lick, a beat. The point is, once you've stumbled upon an idea that you like, an idea that you find appealing in some way… your song's begun. You're on your way.

Here's the cool thing about improvisation: it's meant to be an adventure! When you allow yourself to be playful and relaxed, you're able go in new directions, venture into untried musical landscapes, explore unfamiliar lyrical territory. Of course, like any journey into the unknown, there are inherent risks. You might suddenly stumble over a nugget of lyrical gold, but you're just as likely to find yourself stuck in a melodic cul-de-sac or starve in a lyrical drought for lack of a good rhyme. But don't let that stop you. Keep going. Don't quit! When you improvise, you're experimenting – like a mad scientist combining different chemicals - and in the process you're guaranteed to make plenty of mistakes (try not to blow anything up). And that's where the fun starts, because some of those inadvertent mistakes can wind up being your best ideas. The *hard* part is recognizing them. In fact, *one of the most valuable attributes of any songwriter is the ability to recognize their useful mistakes*.

This idea of 'exploring new territory' while improvising and recognizing those 'useful mistakes' bears repeating.

Whenever I sit down with an instrument or word processor to improvise, I do my best to relax and simply enjoy the experience – to have fun. But at the very same time, I'm also consciously striving to *'try new stuff'*, to do things I haven't done before, to try chord progressions that are unfamiliar, to use different voicings, or unexpected lyrical phrasings or rhyme schemes, or tell a story in an atypical way or from an unusual perspective. No doubt this experimental approach can yield plenty of unusable junk, *but* if you are patient with yourself and try to withhold your hyper-critical judgement (at least early on), *eventually* one of those 'mistakes' will turn out to be the perfect basis of a new song.

Every successful songwriter has experienced a point early on, while writing a new song, where they thought to themselves, 'Wow, this idea really sucks!' But as often as not, that song idea, which at first seemed surprising or slightly jarring or downright *weird*, turns out to be the very thing that makes the song original and unique, or even great! Traveling the safe, boring route will tend to result in a safe, boring song. Take a chance. Try something new.

Once, a few years back, while working on a kids musical titled, 'Smelly Feet' – a children's musical that really *stinks!* - I was challenged with writing a song for the main character, Pete, who had an unfortunate case of 'smelly feet'.

Pete and his best friend Danny kept doing experiments in an attempt to cure Pete's smelly feet, including rubbing honey all over Pete's feet (bad idea) or leaving Pete's sneakers outside overnight to air out. The experiments failed – Pete's feet still stunk – but Pete acquired a slow moving pet after finding a snail had climbed into one of his sneakers, overnight. Pete, despondent over his odiferous dilemma, grows rather fond of his new pet, Slimey, and begins confiding in him. (Patience, the point is coming)

At first, Slimey, was merely a prop in the show, not even a character, but as I thought about Pete and his growing affection for Slimey, it occurred to me that it might not be such a crazy idea to have Pete sing a love song to his pet snail. Actually, at first, to be honest, it *did* seem like a crazy idea, but the more I considered it, the more I thought it was worth a try.

I'm relaying this anecdote because throughout the writing of the song, Ode to a Snail (I Like You), I *continually* doubted myself, thinking, 'This is a really stupid idea! This is never going to work. Who sings a love song to a snail?'. The song turned out to be the 'heart' of the musical and continues to be a kid-favorite at every performance of the show. It provides an opportunity for the audience to relate to, and empathize with, a not very articulate Pete.

It was a really stupid idea that turned out to be the perfect fit! This anecdote is meant to illustrate and reinforce a fundamental principle of all writing, which is that very often what seem like your dumbest ideas, can actually turn out to be one of your best. The trick is being able to recognize which is which! (Spoiler Alert!: Pete eventually changes his socks, which turn out to be the cause of his 'Smelly Feet'.)

Writing a song is sometimes like completing a crossword puzzle. Once you've filled in the corner word, all you have to do is fill in the rest of the letters to match up with it.

> *"You're never quite sure where the song is going, because you might not find the word to rhyme with the end of the line. You have to find associative meaning to get you there. So it's rather like doing a crossword puzzle backwards. A kind of strange, three-dimensional, abstract crossword puzzle."* - Annie Lennox

Improvising is one of the main tools a songwriter uses to generate ideas. Once you find a good one, that kernel of an idea becomes the *key to solving the rest of your song puzzle*. Now all you have to do is build a song around it!

#3: Follow Your Nose (observe the world around you)

What I'm referring to is drawing inspiration from the world around you. (This relates to lyrical ideas and topics for songs, as well as the music.) Sometimes instead of sitting around waiting for an idea to come to you – you have to go out looking for it. What do I mean? Just that – actively look around for an idea. An analogy in the art world would be 'found' art - collage or sculpture that involves going into the streets and collecting 'found' objects that the artist then rearranges and juxtaposes in interesting ways to create art. For a songwriter, this approach might not require rummaging through junkyards or trash bins for tin cans and light-bulbs (although that's not necessarily a bad idea); you can achieve the same results rummaging through your own world, internal or external – your neighborhood, your house, your closet, your desktop, your bookshelves, your memory, your life.

You don't have to go very far. You can stay seated in your chair. Look around the room and see what catches your eye. A telephone, a picture, a bed, a shadow. Classic songs have been inspired by every one of these ordinary, mundane objects:

Blondie's 'Hanging on the Telephone' [by Jack Lee],
Dylan's 'Lay Lady Lay' (...*lay across my big brass bed.*),
'The Shadow of Your Smile' [by Johnny Mandel and Paul Francis Webster's]
The Classics IV's 'Traces' (*Faded photograph...*), [by Buddy Buie, J. R. Cobb and Emory Gordy, Jr.].

Look around. If your eye settles on a particular object (or color or effect) that's when you should 'follow your nose'. Sniff it out. What does it bring to mind? What does it represent? What theme does it suggest? What kinds of connections can you make using this found object as a jumping off point? Rod Steward sings, 'Every Picture Tells a Story'. So does every object.

Another 'follow-your-nose' approach is to simply open a book: a novel, a biography, a dictionary or rhyming dictionary, a thesaurus, a comic book, the Whole Earth Catalog. Scan and skim until you catch a word, a phrase, an idea, that grabs your attention. One time, in search of a song, I thumbed through my well-worn rhyming dictionary [no real songwriter should be without one – and a thesaurus] and I somehow stumbled upon the word 'hobnobbing'. For some reason it grabbed my attention – made me curious. After much pondering, considering and exploring, I wound up with a catchy and funny song about superheroes and supervillains who drop by my house for a weekend barbecue. The truth is, once I started off with an interesting word like 'hobnobbing', it wasn't that much of conceptual leap to find myself 'Hob-Nobbin' with Batman and Robin'!

All you need is a place to start. A jumping off point. A cornerstone. A first step. Ideas and inspiration are all around us. If it doesn't happen to jump up and smack you on the head, well then, you just might have to go looking for it – eventually, you'll bump into it. So, just look around and 'follow your nose!'.

#4: Stand on Your Head (Change Your Point of View)

I'm using 'Stand on Your Head' as a catch-all phrase that encompasses all the different ways in a which person can actively 'Change Your Point of View'. The importance of changing one's 'Point of View' (P.O.V) is that doing so usually provides you with a fresh perspective and new insight into otherwise familiar situations, settings and relationships. Sameness and over-familiarity can breed boredom and a lack of clarity. By simply changing your P.O.V. you can often notice details and connections that weren't apparent or as obvious from your previous, everyday perspective.

Folks that travel abroad will typically experience a new appreciation for their homeland, seeing it in stark contrast to people and places that are so vastly different.

It's said that every astronaut that has orbited Earth experiences a profound epiphany at viewing our planet from so far away. It's only upon dramatically changing their P.O.V. that they're able to fully comprehend the connectedness and fragility of the human race, surviving as we do clinging to a thin planetary crust and shielded from space by the impossibly faint wisp of an atmosphere. Songwriter, Julie Gold, makes the point with much grace and style in her beautiful classic, 'From a Distance'.

You don't have to don a spacesuit and helmet and blast into the stratosphere to change your P.O.V. (although it sounds like it could be fun!) You don't even have to leave your room.

Changing your P.O.V. can be accomplished with a small dose of imagination. In some respects it's as easy as asking yourself a simple question: What if...?

What if you could fly through space?
What if you could go back in time?
What if furniture and appliances could talk?
What if you were rich - or poor?
What if she loved you?

You can seek a new P.O.V. musically, as well.

What if you only play the black piano keys?
What if you try writing in 3/4 waltz time, or 7/8?
What if you pick up a ukulele instead of a guitar?

What if you try writing a song with only two chords?
What if you tuned your guitar to an open tuning?

The point of 'Standing on Your Head' or 'Changing your Point of View' is to jar you out of familiar ways of looking at life. Seeing from a fresh perspective is how new ideas pop into your head.

On the subject of altering your P.O.V. as a tool for eliciting inspiration, I'm going to risk serious condemnation by addressing a topic that frequently comes up during songwriting seminars I've conducted over the years. It's a taboo topic but in the spirit of full and frank disclosure, I'll offer you what is only my personal P.O.V. on the subject: What about getting high?

There's no denying a long-standing, unfortunately romantic connection between writing and intoxicants. It's difficult to name folks like Jim Morrison, Janis Joplin, or Amy Winehouse and not picture them in an intoxicated state. So, keep in mind these two indisputable facts:

1. You don't have to be shit-faced to write a great song, and...

2. All of the aforementioned musician/writers died prematurely, directly as a result of substance abuse.

Personally, I'm allergic to alcohol, but my song, 'Doint, Doint, It's Just a Little Joint', off my 'Squirrels in the Attic' album, ought to provide an obvious clue as to my personal predilection when it comes to altering one's consciousness.

Anyway, here goes...

Most of my songs were written entirely straight, that is without the aid of any intoxicant. I'd guess about 20% of them were conceived of after having partaken of some herbal remedy, but here's an important point I would make about writing high: While it definitely can alter your P.O.V. and is one way to generate new ideas, be aware that, in my own experience, this approach holds several inherent risks:

1. While you may indeed come up with a slew of what seem like

cool ideas in an altered state, in retrospect, once you've sobered up, most of those ideas may not seem quite as cool as you had previously imagined.

2. While I've definitely come up with some usable ideas in an altered state, I have never – and I repeat, *never* – been able to successfully *finish* a song unless I was 100% straight/sober. In other words, for some folks being high can occasionally serve to generate ideas, but it requires clear-headedness and sober focus to be able to apply the craft of songwriting in order to turn those ideas into a workable song.

3. Any *over*-use of intoxicants will quickly bring you to a point of diminishing returns, which means that any miniscule benefit you may *think* they yield will be quickly and easily outweighed by their negative impact on your physical and mental health and their tendency to significantly reduce your overall energy level, drive and ability to concentrate.

Just to be clear, this is not intended as an endorsement or recommendation or condemnation of mind-altering substances. I am well aware that for a large segment of the population, booze and drugs can have a seriously adverse effect on their lives. I expect anyone reading this to use their own judgement.

If you do happen to indulge, the bottom line is this: if you ever get to a point where you mistakenly believe that you absolutely *can't* write without getting high, you're kidding yourself, and you'll be doing yourself a favor by abstaining for a while.

If you're a teenager reading this, don't be stupid. Use caution. It's a scientific fact that your brains are still developing and I've seen too many young people lose themselves in a cloudy funk of lethargy because they did not yet possess the maturity, self-discipline and common sense to balance their intake and make responsible choices. I'm just telling it like I see it. End of intoxicant lecture. Back to the business of songwriting.

....

If you just open your eyes – and open your mind - you can find inspiration all around you. I've mentioned a few techniques for inviting it in, including listening, improvising, following your nose (observing the world around you), and standing on your head (changing your point of view).

As I mentioned earlier, it's not always necessary to invite inspiration; sometimes an idea can pop into your head when you least expect it – riding a bus, sitting in a restaurant, walking the dog. Some folks come up with song ideas in their dreams, or as they're drifting off to sleep. Again, keeping a pen and notepad handy is a good idea. Jot the stuff down. I've started songs on McDonald's placemats, paper napkins, matchbooks, newspapers, receipts… you name it. I've got draws full of 'em. Every now and then I'll sift through a draw full of sketches and more often than not find something useful to start crafting a song out of.

Either way, whether inspiration lands in your lap or you go out actively searching for it, the goal is to find some kernel of an idea, a lyrical or musical phrase, a guitar lick, a bass pattern, a rhythmic figure, a topic or subject or theme or story that you're inspired to pursue. It can be the flimsiest idea or a single word or song-title, but at some point one of those ideas will possess a certain appeal. It will nag at you and tug at your attention until eventually you find yourself compelled to pursue it. That's when you apply craft and technique to turn your inspiration into a song.

Still stuck? Not sure how to start? Where to begin?

It doesn't matter where or how you start, just that you start. Once you start improvising, writing, playing… once you open the spigot, the good stuff will start to flow. Try committing to writing a song a day. Or go crazy and try writing four or five songs in a single day. It doesn't matter if you fail to reach your quota or if half the songs suck; what *matters* is that you've started writing songs.

Here are a few random suggestions for getting started – there are zillions (possibly even tens of zillions!). Once you get the hang of it, come up with a few of your own. Remember, don't get bogged down with how good or bad stuff is – muffle your inner critic for now – just let the words and music spill out. (You can always clean up the horrible mess later! ;-)

A few random places to start:

1. Buy a bunch of newspapers and magazines and pick a

headline or story that catches your eye.

2. Pick four cards out of a deck and develop a melody based on their numeric value. Or roll a pair of dice.

3. Write a song about your favorite person (that's not your lover or spouse). This is a 'friend' song – not a 'love' song.

4. Sit on a park bench and do some people watching. Make up stories about someone else's life.

5. Write a song about all the things you meant to do – but didn't.

6. Write a song that starts with a question: Why, How, When, etc...?

7. Stroll into your local public library (seriously, they need your business) browse the titles and grab any book off the shelf that strikes your fancy. That's your subject.

8. Ask your friends for song topic suggestions. You'll be surprised at some of the crazy stuff they'll come up with!

9. Conjure up a favorite memory from your childhood. Build a song out of it.

10. Write a song about your favorite historical figure.

The point is you can start a song anywhere. The source material can be important but not nearly as important as what you do with it, how you transform it, how you shape it and make it your own.

With patience, persistence and imagination, any old rock or lump of clay or hunk of wood can be turned into a beautiful work of art. Same with words and notes. All you need to do is start hammering, sculpting and chipping away.

NOTE: A handheld digital recorder, or smartphone, can be a useful sketchpad, although bits of paper provide visual cues that I find easier to sort through. So beware: if you record your song ideas digitally, you need to be extra organized in order to retrieve them easily; otherwise you'll be stuck with a hard-drive filled with hours of noodling and no easy way of accessing it. That means saving the ideas with easy to recognize file-names and putting them into easy to locate folders. These days I often use a small video recorder to grab song ideas; the visual component of the video clips provides more readily identifiable cues for sifting through lots of ideas, as well as a quick reminder of the particular fingering or voicing I used on whatever instrument I was playing.

"Song writing is about getting the demon out of me. It's like being possessed. You try to go to sleep, but the song won't let you. So you have to get up and make it into something, and then you're allowed sleep."

- John Lennon

CRAFT

Inspiration may remain a mystery. What you do with inspiration, once it hits, is what the rest of this handbook is about – the craft of songwriting.

To my mind, the craft of songwriting can be boiled down to one word – *choice*.

The whole point of this book is to provide you with choices, to allow you some measure of control over your creative impulses, to enable you to make *conscious* decisions about where your inspiration will lead or even where it comes from. Inspiration is subconscious. Choice is conscious. Inspiration is the magical aspect of songwriting. Choice is the necessary technical part, the craft of songwriting.

What kinds of choices? Choices like these: What instrument should I write with? What style or musical genre? What key? What chord do I start on? What harmonic vocabulary should I use? What tempo? What rhythmic feel? What type of song structure? What lyrical theme? What sort of rhyme scheme? These are just a few examples of the hundreds of deliberate choices that you can make during the process of writing a song.

Why choose?

Some songs write themselves. This is true. Some songs seem to burst forth, fully formed, from the depths of your psyche, or parachute in from some alternate dimension. When this happens it's best not to get in the song's way. A good idea is to step aside and let inspiration flow unimpeded. Just try to write it all down or record it as quick as you can, so you won't forget. These kinds of songs often possess a raw, unfiltered emotional truth, which is something to be valued in any work of art. When they happen, encourage them. Appreciate them. But, these types of songs are exceedingly rare.

More often than not, you're going to have to work a little harder. You're going to have to wrestle with a lyric or find some way to bend a musical phrase. You're going to have to pick and choose and rearrange and edit and press your imagination to come up with just the perfect word, phrase, melodic line or chord. You may even have to be brave; to challenge yourself to push the envelope, to stretch your mind, to reach deep into yourself and be honest about how you really truly and feel about something – or someone. Songwriting is not always a pursuit for the timid.

We're talking about applying your craft to shape your songs. The real trick is to practice your craft without losing touch of that raw, childlike spirit that is at the soul of every work of art. It's a delicate balancing act, whereby you try your damnedest to control the process, by making choices, while at the same time leaving room for those indefinable moments of inspiration and creativity.

What comes next?

Good question. As I see it, every choice begins with a question. And after considering several possible answers you, the songwriter, get to make a choice, a choice that gradually moves your work-in-progress one step closer to becoming a song.

Do I want to write a rock & roll tune, a folk song, a country ballad, a pop tune?

Will I start on guitar, piano, bass, drum machine?

Am I writing a love song, an historical ballad, a political satire, a tragedy, a fun, get-up-and-dance party-anthem?

Will I write in 4/4 time or try my hand at a 3/4 waltz time? Or throw caution to the wind and take a shot at a ballad in 7/8?

Is this song about a friend, a lover, a relative, the baker, the president, my car, my job, my country, my cat?

NOTE: To hear a great song about a guy and his cat, check out Dan Pelletier's, 'You and Me, Cat'.

Will this tune revolve around a stinging guitar lick, or a gentle acoustic fingerpicking pattern, or a rapid eight-note keyboard part, or a percolating drum loop?

Do I want to start in the familiar key of C? Or shall I attempt a song in a less familiar key (where you'll be more likely to try something different)? Do I want to modulate from one key in the verse to another key in the chorus? Shall I write this song in a minor key or a major key, or switch in the middle?

As I've already said, on rare occasions, some songs write themselves; inspiration flows, you keep out of the way, as best you can, and write it all down. No choices necessary. No tough decisions. No painful editing.

More often than not, though, writing the song is up to you. You still need to make room for inspiration and happy accidents – useful mistakes – but you'll need to be more pro-active in deciding how the song evolves, what shape it takes. You'll need to make choices. A series of them – intertwined with bursts of inspiration. It's a two-handed, alternating process – inspiration, choice, inspiration, choice.

Skate-boarding is how I sometimes picture it. Imagine a kid slaloming down the block, intuitively balanced while exerting a subtle almost subconscious control over his trajectory, occasionally picking up speed with a determined kick off the asphalt. Making a choice is like kicking off in a specific direction, that conscious decision propelling you forward, followed by the exhilarating freedom of effortless momentum, a period of creative flow, until that momentum slows and a well-timed kick propels you forward again. The trick is to get comfortable enough balanced on that skateboard that you not only maneuver with maximum skill, but you do it with style!

CHOICE

The whole rest of this book is about the many *choices* we, as songwriters, get to make about all the different aspects of a song. We'll talk about the many features of song (both musical and lyrical) including idiom, key, tempo, rhythm, rhyme, tone, persona, all the poetic devices such as simile, metaphor and alliteration, we'll discuss things like phrasing and form (song structure). And throughout the discussion of these song elements, we'll keep getting back to the idea that you, the songwriter, get to choose when, and where, and how to make use of all of them.

I've already touched on some of these choices in the preceding series of questions. Most are obvious, a few are not. But I believe it will prove useful to see them listed here, all together, in context, to see how they relate to each other and to get an understanding of how you can use them in combinations to shape a song.

Mostly, my purpose here is to remind you of the breadth and scope of musical and lyrical choices that are yours to make when you sit down to write. There are plenty more not listed here, but this is as good a place as any to start.

Musical Choices (mostly):

- **INSTRUMENT** - *What **instrument** should I start on?* Guitar, Keyboard, Sequencer, Drum Machine. A particular instrument will tend to suggest an idiom.

Unless you tell them otherwise, your fingers may tend to form familiar patterns and chord progressions based on muscle memory and what instrument you happen to be playing. When I sit down at a keyboard, my fingers tend to gravitate to jazz and pop progressions, whereas with an acoustic guitar in hand, I find myself finger-picking country and folk patterns. Plug in an electric guitar and rock riffs spill out. You can often predict what idiom you will tend to explore based on what instrument you pick up, or you can choose to overcome that obvious tendency. Either way, you get to choose.

> *"When you tune your guitar in a different way, it lends itself to a new way of looking at your songwriting."*
> – Sheryl Crow

- **MUSICAL IDIOM** - *What musical idiom (genre, style) do you want to explore?* – A particular idiom (ie. Rock, Pop, Folk, Country, Jazz, R&B, Alternative, Metal) will tend to suggest a specific Harmonic Vocabulary.

I'm sometimes accused of being too eclectic in my songwriting – which I happen to take as a compliment. When it comes to music I'm non-denominational, but that's just me. Plenty of brilliant musicians stick to a specific musical idiom and manage to weave magic, song after song. Then again, some of my favorite artists manage to combine seemingly disparate idioms with amazing results, spawning brand new idioms – the jazz-rock fusion of Steely Dan or Joe Jackson, the folk-jazz of Joni Mitchell. Choose a musical idiom – or don't. Or merge two together. Up to you. Just be aware that whatever musical idiom you wind up working in, will tend to come with its own pre-existing universe of chords and chord progressions – a harmonica vocabulary from which you'll be shaping your song. Not only that, every musical idiom brings with it a world of associations – an atmosphere, an emotional tone - which you can choose to either work with or work against.

Think of the super-slow groove in so many sublime R&B ballads. Even before the lyrics kick in, you can feel something sensuous going on. Or the honky-tonk twang of so many great country tunes. You can almost see that red pickup parked outside the bar, and the red-headed divorcee nursing her drink at the bar, as the pedal-steel guitar plays a pickup to the verse.

- **HARMONIC VOCABULARY** - *What **harmonic vocabulary** best suits this song?* – Every musical idiom has sub-sets of harmonic vocabularies – chord changes (progressions) – which often suggest specific structures to a song.

A basic blues, rock or folk progression might have a familiar three-chord harmonic vocabulary of I, IV, V (or C, F, G in the key of C), but endless variations within each of those idioms can possess a unique and identifiable harmonic vocabulary that will imbue a song with a specific character. The three chord forms of blues and rock, the II, IV progressions and major 7th chords of jazz, the dominant 7th chords of country, the minor chords and modal keys of folk; these are just some of the harmonic vocabularies frequently associated with those idioms.

In fact, some artists possess such a strong identifiable harmonic vocabulary as part of their personal style, that they almost define their own musical idiom. Walter Becker and Donald Fagen of Steely Dan demonstrate a distinct fondness for bi-tonal chords, and fast-shifting, open-voiced suspensions. Gilbert O'Sullivan, makes deft use of half-diminished chords, in his always beautifully crafted songs. The wonderful queen of neo-soul, Sade, works in a slow, hypnotic jazz-soul-pop hybrid idiom defined by mostly minor modal keys and pulsating rhythms that evoke yearning and mystery. A song's harmonic vocabulary sets a distinct mood, and at the same time suggest an overall structure to the song.

- **FORM** – *What type of **form** should your song have?* – A song's form, or structure, refers to the order of its different sections – intro, verse, chorus, bridge, etc... These sections are often referred to, in shorthand, by letters, such as
  - o   ABA (verse/chorus/verse) or
  - o   AB, AB, C, AB (verse/chorus, verse/chorus, bridge, verse/chorus).

The different sections of a song may serve different purposes, for example, verses tend to be filled with descriptive content and narrative, while the chorus may serve to sum up, or underline, those ideas first developed in the verses. And a verse will often have a level of complexity that stands in stark contrast to the simpler, more basic ideas of the chorus.

Just listen to Bruce Springsteen's epic, 'Born in the USA', where verse after verse is jam-packed with vivid imagery, in dramatic contrast to the simple, repetitive chant of the chorus.

This idea of contrast is a crucial element in songwriting – indeed, in all forms of art. Contrast helps differentiate sections of a song and in doing so provides the listener with a kind of roadmap to their musical and lyrical journey. To a listener absorbing new content in a descriptive verse, the return of a familiar chorus can be a satisfying resting place or occasion for emotional release. Being aware of form can help a songwriter figure out what goes *where* and what happens *next*. And as a consequence, being aware of form can help a songwriter shape their audiences' listening experience.

PARTS OF A SONG

Intro / Verse / Pre-Chorus / Chorus / Bridge / Coda (End)

I'll try to keep this section short because most of it's pretty obvious. I plan to address some of the stuff that's not.

Intro – You've gotta start somewhere. These days, most intros tend to be short instrumental-only riffs or grooves that move you quickly to the first verse. But in the Broadway show tune tradition of the 50's and 60's, intros with music and lyrics played a crucial role in setting up the storyline that was inevitably fleshed out in the whole of the song itself. Unlike most of today's songs, the music in those intros was often very distinct from the body of the song, but served to set the stage musically as well as dramatically. Songs like West Side Story's 'Maria' [Leonard Bernstein & Stephen Sondheim] and My Fair Lady's 'I Could Have Danced All Night' [Alan Jay Lerner and Frederick Loewe] did just that while also providing a natural transition from spoken dialogue to the main body of the song.

Only a decade later, the Beatles (who incidentally covered the Broadway show tune, 'Till There Was You', from Meredith Willson's Music Man), continued that tradition by composing complex intros to some of their most beloved tunes. Check out the intro to Lennon & McCartney's beautiful, 'If I Fell'. What's remarkable about the intro to, 'If I Fell', is that it not only poses the primary question, 'If…' that sets up the lyric, but the music passes through several key changes before landing surprisingly and satisfyingly on the main key of the song. The body of the song is one of their most beautiful, but the intro alone is mind-blowing!

Paul and John do it again in 'Do You Want to Know a Secret'. This time, the intro starts in a minor key which serves as a dramatic way to surprise the listener with the sudden switch to a major key on the first chord of the verse.

And what about their thrilling intro to, 'Help!'? One of my personal favs, this intro, distinct from the entire rest of the song, is so raw and emphatic, with its shouting cry for help that it's the musical and lyrical equivalent of pulling a fire-alarm.

But like I just said, today – and really for most of the last half century - most intros are quickly identifiable guitar licks or bass riffs, musically identical to the body of the song, and mostly there to grab your attention and announce that the song is about to start in a measure or two. A song like Mark Knofler's 'Money for Nothing' [Dire Straits], that begins with Sting singing about how he wants his MTV, would be the exception, not the rule.

And why do you need to know this? You don't. But it just might give you something to think about the next time you sit down to write. If it helps to expand your understanding of song structure and the ways in which different parts of a song can function, well, that's not a bad thing.

Verse – I don't have to tell you what a verse is, but if you want me to keep typing I'll just say that it's the part of a song where you tell most of your story. It's your exposition, the section where you get to elaborate on and expand on your topic; as opposed to the chorus where you typically summarize, reiterate and underline the main idea of your song.

Pre-Chorus - Some songs have a two-part verse, in which the second part of the verse leads inevitably into the chorus. That second part of the verse usually serves as a transitional section between the main verse and the chorus and often its musical identity is very distinct from the main part of the verse. If the second part of a verse is especially unique and distinct from the first part, it's often referred to as a pre-chorus, which aptly describes its function as a build-up to the chorus. Dramatically its function is akin to the wind-up of a pitch. Tension builds, here it comes... Chorus! In Adele's, 'Someone Like You' [Adele and Dan Wilson], after a double verse, something changes, musically and lyrically, when she begins to sing,

I hate to turn up out of the blue, uninvited...

Tension mounts, she's leading us somewhere, preparing us for what's about to happen next. What happens next is the chorus. And it feels good once we get there.

A similar thing happens in Lana Del Rey's, 'Video Games' [Lana Del Rey and Justin Parker], when towards the end of each verse she sings,

It's you, it's you, it's all for you. Everything I do.
I tell you all the time...

The Pre-Chorus connects the verse to the chorus, but it does more than just connect, it prepares the listener for what's coming. It plays a crucial transitional role leading the listener logically, dramatically and inevitably to the chorus.

Chorus - This is where you summarize, emphasize, repeat and underline what you just spent all that time explaining in the verses. Verses are where you carefully, sometimes in great detail, explain to your listener what your song is all about. The Chorus, especially in a pop song, is where you bang them over the head with a hammer, to drive the point home. Choruses tend to be simpler than verses, but that's not always the case. Some choruses can be quite complex and raise more questions than they resolve. Jimmy Webb's majestic, but seemingly inexplicable, 'MacArthur Park', is a case in point. There's nothing simple about the chorus, in fact the structure of the entire seven minute and twenty five second song defies all convention, which makes sense when you learn that, according to Webb, the song is really an excerpt from a cantata, he had composed, a classical song form with much greater variation than most contemporary songs.

Bridge – This is a section in many songs that departs from the verse and chorus. Sometimes called 'the middle eight' (if it's eight measures long), a bridge provides new material that serves as a contrast to, and release from, the musical ideas already established in the verses and chorus. Check out tunes such as The Beach Boy's 'Wouldn't it be Nice' [Brian Wilson, Tony Asher, Mike Love], Paul Simon's 'America' and so many early classic Beatles tunes like, 'And I Love Her', 'I Should Have Known Better' and 'I Saw Her Standing There', to name just a few [Lennon & McCartney]. All of these songs have middle sections, bridges, that offer the listener something distinctly different, both musically and lyrically, than the rest of the song. Typically, the bridge is still addressing the same subject matter and working in the same harmonic realm, but offering up a new perspective, a change of pace that makes the return of the verse and/or chorus that much more satisfying.

Coda (End) – Also called an Outro or a Tag, this is the bit at the very end of your song. It's how you finish. Usually, it repeats material, a line or phrase, already heard somewhere in the body of the song, with some slight variation. Think of the end of 'Somewhere Over the Rainbow' [Harold Arlen and E.Y. Harburg]

> *If happy little bluebirds fly beyond the rainbow,*
> *Why, oh why can't I?*

This coda uses material we've already heard in the bridge, but transforms it at the very end with a delicate ascending melodic line.

Some songs end abruptly, or by gradually slowing down (called a 'ritard'), or by fading out over a looping measure or two ('fade-out', also referred to as a 'ride-out'). Many of these are arranging devices that are tacked on after the song itself has been written, but just as often they're composed as an integral part of the song.

Remember, all these terms are merely convenient ways of referring to different sections of a song, but let me stop you right here, before we go any further. Because, with all this talk of song sections and bridges and pre-choruses, etc..., this is something important you need to understand:

A song doesn't have to have a bridge.

A song doesn't have to have an intro – or outro!

A song doesn't have to have a pre-chorus.

A song doesn't even have to have a damn chorus!

O.K., there's gotta be something left, so you might as well call it a verse. So yes, a song needs a verse, if nothing else. But even there, plenty of songs have verses that contain a musical/lyrical hook packed inside of 'em, that essentially functions as a mini-chorus. Listen to Bruce Springsteen's 'Thunder Road'. Can you find where the verses end, and is there even anything resembling a chorus that repeats? I can't find it. Or does the fevered verse build into an emotional climax beginning with the lines,

> *'...roll down the window*
> *And let the wind blow back your hair*
> *Well the night's busting open*
> *These two lanes will take us anywhere...*

and conclude with the repetition of the hook, 'Thunder Road', echoed and underlined by Clarence Clemons' tenor saxophone?

Sometimes songs just flow, with an internal logic of their own. You don't always have to overthink it. The only reason I'm even bothering to cover the traditional terms for parts of a song is to remind you of the options available to you; to open your eyes, ears and minds to the endless variety of song structures and forms, so that once you're aware of all that variety, you can pick and choose, or choose not to use, any of those song parts for your own songs.

Listen to the astonishing, 'At Seventeen', by Janis Ian. I say astonishing because it's so beautifully written, and so dizzyingly honest and so transcendently soulful, that it's astonishing (a) that such a sublime song was every written and (b) that something so excellent, and seemingly non-commercial, ever made it onto a radio playlist. That fact that it became a #1 record on the Billboard charts is one of those rare instances where sheer quality defies the odds by rising to the top of an industry that is more accustomed to worshipping mediocre trends, than rewarding stunning originality!

Anyway, where was I? Oh, right – we were talking about the 'parts of a song'.

Where's the chorus in this song? Is there one? Or would you describe it as a bridge? Or a B section of the verse? And where does the second section actually end? Because it seems to keep on going, its melody and lyric continually unfolding towards its surprising, yet inevitable, resolution.

The point is, I don't care what you call the sections of this or any song. The only value in analyzing a song in this way is simply to familiarize you with the many different ways a song can be structured and then to immediately stress the idea that you don't have to follow a typical verse, chorus, bridge structure. You can if you want. But as far as I'm aware, there is no actual law on the books that says you have to follow a particular song structure or that you have to follow any song structure at all. If familiarity with a conventional form helps by providing you with more choices at a certain juncture in your own song, that's great. Hmmmm... should I try putting a bridge here? Is this a good place to extend the verse with a pre-chorus? Otherwise, just keep writing, follow your instincts. If you've fed your brain with enough good music, your inner ear will tell you what to do next.

> *"I write a lot from instinct. But as you're writing out of instinct, once you reach a certain level as a songwriter, the craft is always there talking to you in the back of your head...that tells you when it's time to go to the chorus, when it's time to rhyme. Real basic craft... it's second nature."* - Janis Ian

Here are some more examples of songs by a couple of damn good (ie. great) songwriters who've essentially thrown conventional song structure out the window. You should check 'em out.

First try good ol' Sir Paul McCartney's, 'Uncle Albert Admiral Halsey', which consists of at least four unique song ideas stitched together into a inexplicably catchy song-quilt.

And what of the masterful, Brian Wilson's, 'Good Vibrations', perhaps the greatest record of all time (definitely I.M.H.O.)? By my count the song consists of at least five distinct musical sections.

And then, of course, there's Freddie Mercury's 'Bohemian Rhapsody', a mini rock opera with so many dramatically different and distinct song sections to it that I gave up counting after six.

Without boring the hell out of you, I'll say it again: learn to hear the various ways in which other writers have cobbled together their songs using different song sections. But don't obsess over it. Expose yourself to it, assimilate it, and then stop worrying about it. If in the process of writing your own song, an idea pops into your head and you ask yourself, 'hmmmm… I wonder if it would be O.K. to do this, in this section?' the answer is always YES!

And now let us continue identifying even more parts of a song, which you will then be encouraged to forget about immediately afterwards, because this stuff is going to be second nature to pretty much any one reading this book.

Hooks, Riffs & Licks

Hooks, Riffs & Licks are musician slang that refer to memorable parts of a song. As I've just indicated, you already know what they are, but for the benefit of any vacationing Aliens or Artificial Intelligence that has suddenly achieved sentience, I'll attempt to define them (in hopes that they'll then look favorably upon our pitiable race, instead of enslaving us all to work in their plasma energy factories).

A hook is something on the wall that you hang your hat or coat on. If the hook wasn't there, your coat or hat or valor sweater would fall to the ground in a crumpled pile on the floor.

In a song, a hook refers to an especially memorable section of the song, usually the chorus, that stands out in such a way, and has such an immediately identifiable quality to it, that it, essentially, makes the song. Without it, the song would fall to the ground in a crumpled pile on the studio floor.

A good hook is, by definition, satisfying to the ear and instantly recognizable after only one listen, such that the listener longs to hear it again – and again – and again.

A hook is also a sharp, barbed, curved piece of metal, designed to capture curious fish. Similarly, a musical hook is designed to capture the listener's attention (but not eat 'em – usually).

But a hook doesn't have to necessarily be the chorus; a striking instrumental phrase can serve as a hook, a compelling and repeated lyric towards the end of a verse can serve the same important function.

In Tracy Chapman's entrancing, 'Fast Car', there is no conventional pop hook, but there's something hypnotic about the repetitive guitar figure that serves as both the intro to the song and accompaniment to the verses. You could call that guitar figure a hook. The 'B' section of the song, *'So remember when we were driving, driving in your car...'* is not exactly a chorus, but has more impact with each repetition. You could call that a hook. And then there's the evocative title phrase, *'You've got a fast car...'*, which is repeated a total of six times in the song. That's definitely a hook.

Again, we're just naming things here. Reviewing common terminology. You don't sit down and write a hook. You sit down and write a song, and then sit back and say, 'hmmm... pretty nice hook, right there. Not bad. Not bad at all.'

Riffs and Licks and Hooks are almost synonymous in that they all refer to an especially catchy section of a song. Although, while a hook can refer to an entire chorus, riffs and licks generally refer to a shorter instrumental segment; the classic guitar lick in the Beatles' 'Day Tripper', the iconic sax line in Gerry Rafferty's 'Baker Street'. But realize that at this point, we're edging into the realm of instrumental arrangement and record production, areas which overlap with the realm of song-writing. Plenty of great guitar licks or keyboard riffs were created after the fact and grafted onto an existing song, but just as many songs started off with, and were then built upon, a catchy lick or riff.

In these days of digital audio workstations (DAW's) and easy access to multi-track digital studios, the recording studio itself becomes an instrument, and beats and grooves and sampled loops all become source material for writing a song.

Regardless of what name you give it, or what instrument you composed it on, the basic idea is the same, you want to create something that grabs the listener by the ear.

Why am I telling you this?

To give you one more strategy for writing your song. If your word-processor's not doing it for you, pick up a guitar instead, or sit at a keyboard or drum-machine and start messing around until you come up with a cool riff, or awesome lick, or wicked beat, or tasty groove or killer loop that gets you jazzed. All you need to do to start a song is to come up with the tiniest kernel of a good idea – and take it from there.

- **KEY** – *What key will you compose your song in?* – Choosing a key may seem a neutral choice, but on the contrary, what key you decide to write in can have a profound impact on how your song evolves.

It's easy to start writing a song in the key your hands are most accustomed to playing, on whatever instrument is at hand. If I pick up a guitar, my hands will usually gravitate to playing in the key of 'G' (lots of open strings in G); on a piano I might lazily improvise in 'C' (none of those pesky black keys). That's fine, zillions of excellent songs have been written in those keys. But there are two reasons I usually (not always) make a conscious effort to resist that default approach:

(1) Writing a song in an unfamiliar key, can help you avoid the over-used note patterns and chord changes that your hands will tend to reach for, automatically. You're more likely to discover new sounds, different voicings, new chord progressions and fresh approaches to melody, simply by virtue of finding yourself in new and unexplored musical territory. Sometimes the familiar can be comfortable and reassuring, which is perfectly fine, but *sometimes* the familiar can just be plain boring. If you're striving for originality and hoping to create something new, try getting out of your comfort zone a bit and see what happens.

(2) Everyone's vocal range is different, and the key a song is written in will inevitably play an important role in how a particular song sits within a person's vocal range. My vocal range is about 2 ½ octaves and unconsciously, regardless of what key I'm composing in, my voice has a tendency to explore both the upper

and lower boundaries of that range, even while it plants itself squarely in the middle of its range for the bulk of the melody.

My vocal range doesn't change but the relative harmonic background does, depending on the key I'm singing in. This means that the middle of my vocal range – where most of my melody usually lays – will likely concentrate on different parts of the diatonic scale, depending on the key. In other words, singing in a new key will tend to force me to place my melodies in a different part of the scale, imparting a slightly different character to those melodies.

So, for example, instead of always starting on the 1st note of a scale (the tonic or root), a key change might prompt me to concentrate a melody on the 4th or 5th. The same shift will pertain to the top and bottom of my range. I'm still singing the same high notes at the edge of my vocal range, but in one key that note may be a 3rd and in another key that high note might be a 7th. A big difference.

Juxtaposing my relatively limited vocal range onto a new key will usually compel me to explore new melodies in different parts of the scale. All of which keeps writing fresh and can help you avoid redundancy.

Then again, there have been occasions where I purposefully shifted a song's key until I was able to take maximum advantage of a particular quality of my voice at the top or bottom of my vocal range. When I wrote my song, 'Under the Weather', I strived to match the intimacy of the lyric, so I purposely pitched it towards the mid-upper range of my voice which allowed me to sing with an almost spoken, slightly breathy quality. By comparison I chose a key for my song, 'You're Invisible', that allowed me to sing at the slightly gravely, lower edge of my vocal range, which well suited the dark tone of the lyric.

Like it or not, your song is going to start out in one key or another. You can let it happen by accident, or you can make that decision on purpose.

- **RHYTHM/TEMPO (BEAT, GROOVE)** – *What rhythmic groove or feel should your song have? How fast? How slow? What time signature?* – Rhythm, tempo, time signature (4/4, 3/4, 7/8, etc...), beat, groove, feel... all these rhythmic time elements will have a profound effect on what your song becomes.

A fast tempo can impart an aggressive energy and freneticism to a song; a slow tempo may impart a moody, contemplative, often dramatic tone. And within the broad spectrum of different tempos, a song's groove can instantly place it within recognizable idioms all of which come accompanied by their own associations which will instantly attach themselves to your song. An uptempo rock-a-billy shuffle, a mid-tempo rock anthem, a slow, sultry R&B ballad… each type of groove will evoke a certain feel and expectation in the ears and mind of the listener. A four-on-the-floor dance groove at 120 BMP's instantly encourages the listener to get up and move. A slow reggae groove with a bass drum on 2 and 4 (instead of the more typical 1 and 3) can instantly conjure up a relaxed island feel unless, of course, it's co-opted by the Police to expound on their brilliant musical hybridization of reggae rock and jazz. See 'Walking on the Moon' [by Sting / The Police].

Writing a song with a 3/4 time signature (waltz time) will immediately differentiate it from the more commonly used 4/4. Listen to the truly fantastic, 'Fairytale Of New York' [Jem Finer and Shane MacGowan of the Pogues]. The track starts out in 4/4, but the main section of the song kicks into a 3/4 uptempo, Irish waltz that serves as the perfect setting for this foul-mouthed, and deliriously joyful, Christmas love song. Experimenting with different rhythms, tempos, beats, time-signatures and grooves will inevitably steer you into making new musical discoveries as you find ways to merge your own musical identity into a unique rhythmic framework. And having some understanding of the differences between those rhythmic frameworks will provide you with a powerful tool for shaping your songs.

- **INITIAL EVENTS** – *What's a good chord to start the verse or chorus on? What's a good note to start the melody on?* – First impressions, first steps, opening lines… those initial events set the tone, or grab your attention demanding that you listen to what comes next. It's never a bad idea to give them a second thought.

Sameness and familiarity play an important role in music. Our ears are accustomed to hearing certain chord progressions, certain familiar musical structures. Musical idioms exist because collections of songs share similar, recognizable features. As songwriters we can take advantage of that familiarity by tapping into an idiom's recognizable progressions and structures. But at the very same time we can take even further advantage of those familiar patterns – by breaking them.

Do all your songs begin with a I chord (the tonic. Example: C in the key of C)? Do all your melodies start on the 3rd note of the scale? (E in the key of C). Do all your lyrics begin on the downbeat of the 1st measure? Are all your choruses in the same key as your verses? Newsflash!: They don't have to be! Try starting your song with a II chord instead (Dm in the key of C). Try starting your melody on a major 7th (B in the key of C). Try beginning your lyric on the 2nd beat of the measure, instead of the 1st. Try shifting your chorus to a brand new key and then see what you come up with harmonically in order to work yourself back to the verse. Your initial instincts might work out fine. It's worked for you before, and it'll probably work for you again. But trying something new at the outset is guaranteed to yield different and interesting results. They won't always be successful, but sometimes they'll be just what you were looking for – and you won't know unless you try.

This try-something-different approach really applies to every single step along the creative path. I'm simply emphasizing the idea, here, in regards to initial events and the beginnings of songs and song sections, because those are the places that a new approach will tend to be most visible (or audible). In reality, I'm always looking for new, original ways of expressing a musical or lyrical idea, but I never lose sight of the fact that I'm typically working within familiar idioms or structures and so that anything new will still tend to relate to the idiom it's written in. As a writer, I'm always trying to surprise the listener. And usually that surprise comes about because the listener is expecting the song to go to a familiar place. The creative challenge is taking your listener to a brand new place that's still a recognizable part of the journey.

In Diane Warren's exquisite ballad, 'Un-Break My Heart', when Toni Braxton sings the title line leading to the chorus, there's a dramatic and unexpected key change from Bm to Dm. It's not so much a key change, as it is a key *leap*, into another vocal and *emotional* register. Though unanticipated by the listener, Diane carefully sets up the key change with a chord progression and ascending melody that, in retrospect, make the surprise jump sound almost inevitable, and yet still exhilarating every time you hear it. I don't know for sure, but I strongly suspect that Ms. Warren, one of the most successful songwriters on the planet, more than likely made a conscious decision to change keys at that particular point in order to elevate the chorus. Either way, it's a brilliant piece of songwriting.

When I sat down to write the song, 'Sometimes I Forget', I recall resisting the impulse to start the verse on the tonic (or the I chord; C in the key of C). I already had most of the lyrics to a first verse…

We squabble and fight.
We turn out the light.
We toss and turn all through the night…

The word *squabble* is what got me committed to finishing the song. And after thinking about if for a while, it also held a clue for me to figure out what my first chord would be. That word, along with the first three lines of the song suggested a kind of tension that wasn't relieved until the following line

But come the dawn, our arms are wrapped around each other tight.

There's one chord in particular which almost by definition is filled with tension, and that's the diminished chord.

You don't have to study jazz harmony to hear this, you just need a pair of ears (or at least one). In technical terms, a diminished chord is a triad made of two minor thirds. In layman's terms, it's the chord you hear in a movie soundtrack while the killer stalks their prey.

The innate tension evoked by a diminished chord also makes it an ideal transitional chord, because it desperately wants to resolve somewhere – anywhere! That knowledge is what inspired me to start the verse with a diminished chord, instead of the tonic (I) or dominant (V) chords that most songs begin with. It took a bit of tweaking and massaging to find a melody and subsequent chord progression that made it all work, but as far as I was concerned, the results were worth the effort. And I wouldn't have bothered to expend the effort in the first place if it weren't for the fact that I was consciously trying to do something different at the beginning of the song. Try it. You'll be pleased with the results.

Lyrical Choices (mostly):

- **THEME** – *What's this song about?* Whether you realize it or not, your song is about something. And as a songwriter, the sooner you figure out what your song is about, the easier it'll be to complete it.

A song can be about absolutely anything. Having said that, it should come as no surprise to learn that about 96% of all the songs ever written in the history of the world are 'love' songs. (note: I totally made that figure up but I'm sure it's not far off). Let's assume that the 'love' song category also includes 'hate' songs or 'my-baby-done-me-wrong' songs. That still leaves a truck load of categories that typically deal with different aspects of personal relationships (friends, siblings, parents); life events (birth, youth, aging, health, death, separation); history, documentary & social commentary (history, biography, journalism, current events, politics, trends); religion & philosophy (worship, advice, ideas, motivation, aphorisms, warnings); and all kinds of other stuff (animals, places and things).

The above incomplete list of topics/themes is there, in part, to remind you that you really can write a song about anything. I've written my fair share of love songs, but I've also written songs featuring talking furniture, superheroes, snow-days, a snail, my favorite pillow, the Hudson River and the financial crash of 2008. Come to think of it, the songs about the snail and my favorite pillow were also love songs in a way, but that's beside the point.

The real point I want to emphasize is that that the sooner you figure out what your song is actually about, the easier it will be to complete. Once you've figured out what your song is about, you can start asking yourself questions about the topic at hand. The answers to those questions will become your song.

Here's how it works: As soon as I figure out what my song is about, *I ask myself dozens of questions* pertaining to the topic. What are the key points? At this stage, I'm something of a reporter

– Who? What? Where? When? And Why? Those questions tend to cover the most interesting and relevant areas of the subject, and the answers they yield provide me with the basic material for my song. Using those answers, I'll write down lists of words or phrases that seem the most relevant, the most meaningful. I'll fill a page or more with content.

Then, I start to rhyme. I'll generate couplet after couplet using that list of words and phrases as my source material.

> NOTE: I tend to overwrite, which is an approach that works for me. I'll usually write many more couplets or verses to a song than I can practically use. This has the potential to generate lots of useful ideas, allowing you to then pick out the best. But that's also the downside to overwriting, namely that at some point, in the process of picking out the best stuff, you're forced to whittle down those ideas to a manageable size. And that means bouts of fierce and brutal self-editing, a kind of creative triage whereby you destroy some really nice bits of writing in order to better serve the entire piece as a whole. It's not an easy task. There's a very unpleasant term writers sometimes deploy describing this process, known as 'killing your babies'. Horrible, but apt. 'Don't get married to your material' is a less violent description (depending on your marriage), but the point is the same. Good writing often requires deft use of a scalpel or switchblade. Now and then a blowtorch is in order.

This process of asking questions about your material, and using those answers to generate new content, developing couplets (which you turn into whole stanzas, verses, choruses etc…) and then editing that content, can go on for a while. Basically, repeat until done.

I'll be reiterating this basic idea throughout this book. It works for me – not always, but most of the time. Feel free to adjust the recipe to suit your own style of writing.

In a pinch, it's somewhere to start. If you find yourself stuck in the middle of a song, ask yourself questions about what you've already written – *interrogate* your material. More often than not, the answers to those questions will provide you with clues about where to go next.

Once you know what your song is about, here's one thing to keep in mind: it's a good idea to make sure the rest of your content is consistent with that theme. Every line that relates to your theme reinforces your basic premise and will make your song that much stronger and more coherent – *most* of the time.

Here's one of the strange and wonderful things about songwriting: sometimes you don't figure out what your song is *really* about until many years later – if at all.

And not to confuse the issue, but at the end of the day, what your song really means is not ultimately up to you – it's up to the listener. They're the ones that get to decide. How 'bout them apples?

> *"Often I don't know what the song means until it's finished. Sometimes months later. I don't think that's bad. It implies that I don't know what I'm doing, but I think if you're able to follow your instincts, then that's knowing what you're doing."* - David Byrne

- **TONE / ATTITUDE / PERSONA** – *What's the tone or attitude of the song? What type of persona or character does the singer adopt when performing the song?* Regardless of its topic or theme, a song possesses an attitude or tone. That attitude can be serious or light, wry or deadpan, comedic or sad, gentle or angry, poetic or literal, preachy or reassuring, boastful or self-deprecating. The lyrics alone don't tell the whole story; it's a combination of both the lyrics and the music, plus the added ingredient of performance playing a crucial part.

An overriding tone or attitude provides a crucial context for your lyrics and underlying music, and can serve to reinforce or even contradict the inherent meaning of the text.

> NOTE: This is the first time I'm mentioning performance as part of the songwriting mix. It's not always integral to the process, but it usually is. In the case where a singer-songwriter is composing songs to sing themselves, performance plays an obvious role in terms of how notes are sung, and lyrics are phrased, and sentiments are expressed. But even when writing a song for someone else to perform, the potential for how that song will eventually be performed should always be in the back, or even the forefront, of the writer's mind. Ultimately the writing of a song and its eventual performance are inextricably linked.

Consider a song like Willie Dixon's classic blues boast, 'Hoochie Coochie Man', made popular in recent times by Muddy Water and Eric Clapton, among others. Here's a verse:

The gypsy woman told my mother
Before I was born
I got a boy child's comin'
He's gonna be a son of a gun
He gonna make pretty women's
Jump and shout
Then the world wanna know
What this all about
But you know I'm him
Everybody knows I'm him
Well you know I'm the hoochie coochie man
Everybody knows I'm him

Or consider a more recent homage to that song and others like it, George Thorogood's (and the Destroyers) exuberant, 'Bad to the Bone':

On the day I was born
The nurses all gathered 'round
And they gazed in wide wonder
At the joy they had found

The head nurse spoke up
Said "leave this one alone"
She could tell right away
That I was bad to the bone

Both of these songs (and not to take anything away from the terrific, George Thorogood, but for all practical purposes they're essentially the same song) rely on an unabashed attitude of fearlessness and confident self-assuredness.

Just for the hell of it, here's one more song steeped in that very same tradition of self-confident exuberance, this time written by the superb, Natalie Merchant; a verse from her song, 'Wonder':

Doctors have come from distant cities
Just to see me
Stand over my bed
Disbelieving what they're seeing
They say I must be one of the wonders
Of god's own creation
And as far as they can see they can offer
No explanation

Be sure to search out Natalie's recording of this song. Even though she's singing a song that's part of a well tread tradition of exaggerated boasting, she imparts her own individual tone to her song. The character, or persona, that she assumes in singing the lyrics is not just being boastful about her miraculous birth; in some ways, the persona she sings with is just as incredulous and astonished at the wonder of her birth as everyone else!

> NOTE: Here's another terrific song following in this time-honored tradition, marked by a state of egocentric bliss: Have a listen to New Middle Class's song, 'I Was Born', [by Mike Borok, sung by Barbara Borok].

There's a deep connection between performance and writing. When you perform a song, there's a degree of acting involved. The singer is assuming a role and delivering the song lyrics in the guise of that character. That character's voice – embittered elder, irrepressible youth, knowing sage, unreliable narrator – will have a significant impact not only on how a song is sung but on how your song lyrics evolve in the first place. Understanding that character's voice early on will help you discover how that character speaks and what kinds of lyrics come naturally to them.

Another good way to illustrate the power of tone is to show how it can work in contrast, by juxtaposing a comic lyric with a supposedly serious attitude.

Sometime in the late '80's, I was somewhat taken aback to learn that a punk band named, Half Man, Half Biscuit, had released a best-selling EP including a track entitled, 'The Bastard Son of Dean Friedman' [by Nigel Blackwell / Half Man Half Biscuit]. This was some cause for concern. But, after doing the math, I concluded, to my great relief, that in order for me to have sired, Nigel Blackwell (lead singer and songwriter for Half Man, Half Biscuit), I would have had to have done so when I was seven years old. I was admittedly a precocious child, but not *that* precocious.

In any case, despite my respect and admiration for Nigel's impressive songwriting skills, I set about to exact my revenge. I had in mind to tell the ridiculous and sordid tale of Nigel's dubious origins, which had resulted in him becoming, Half Man, Half Biscuit.

Obviously, this took place in a bakery. But while crafting the song, filled with awful puns and innuendough, I made a very conscious decision to couch the lyric in the context of what I imagined to be a traditional tragic folk ballad.

The attitude and tone of 'A Baker's Tale' was meant to be delivered with sincerity and pathos, even while the lyric told an absurd and impossible tale. Somehow, the juxtaposition works. The earnest tone superimposed on top of the inane lyric provides the audience with just enough suspension of belief for them to actually visualize this most unlikely conception. Laughs (and groans) abound!

Here are the first two verses of, 'A Baker's Tale', to give you a small sample of my culinary revenge [NOTE: Do check out the full track, but before you do, be sure to listen to Nigel's aforementioned masterpiece, 'The Bastard Son...', first! ;-)]:

Once there was a humble baker
Who spent all day making buns and cakes and
Rolls and loaves of bread and muffins
And he loved his work but it wasn't enough and…

He longed to offer up his heart
to not just any tart,
but one of substance and of virtue
but suitable candidates were oh so few.

    Nigel Blackwell, pray please do tell,
    How could your parents risk it?
    Baker's son, born of a bun
    Half a man, half a biscuit

He gently took her from the oven
Her sweet scent set off waves of loving
His eyes beheld her flakey crust.
He thought, "I mustn't… but I must!"

Alas, Nigel's dad could not resist her
He held her close and then he kissed her
Before another word was uttered
His momma's buns were buttered

    Nigel Blackwell, pray please do tell,
    How could your parents risk it?
    Baker's son, born of a bun
    Half a man, half a biscuit

It's difficult to know what to say after all that surreal song-slinging, except this: tone, attitude and persona matter.

- **PERSPECTIVE (P.O.V) / PERSON** – *Who are you singing about or to? Me, You or Them?* In grammar, 'person' refers to the perspective or P.O.V. (point of view) of the pronoun being used. Choosing a song's perspective can have tremendous impact on how your listeners relate to your story.

A 'first person' lyric will employ a lot of the pronouns: I, we, me, us, my, mine, our and ours. You're speaking about your personal experience and expressing your own feelings. A lot of powerful songs are written in 'first person', potentially offering a glimpse directly into the mind and heart of the author. Then again, if you use too many 'I's and 'me's in your songs you run the risk of self-obsession.

Here's a short list of 'first person' songs that just happen to begin with the word 'I' or 'We':

> I Can't Get No Satisfaction [The Rolling Stones]
> I Am a Rock [Paul Simon / Simon & Garfunkle]
> I Am Woman [Helen Reddy]
> We Are the World [Michael Jackson, Lionel Richie]
> We Are the Champions [Freddie Mercury / Queen]

Got it?

A 'second person' lyric will tend to employ the pronouns: you, your, and yours. You're aiming your words and thoughts directly at the listener, describing things as you see 'em. Think of the many love songs (or fuck you songs) - that focus on the second person 'you' in their lyric, the object of the writer's affections (or contempt). Directly addressing your listener in a lyric is sure to grab their attention. You just have to decide what it is you want to tell them.

Carly Simon's song, "You're So Vain" is a good example of a 'second person' point of view. It's all about *you* (or Mick Jagger or Warren Beatty or whichever self-absorbed jerk she was dating at the time.):

> *You walked into the party like you were walking onto a yacht.*
> *Your hat strategically dipped below one eye. Your scarf it was apricot.*
> *You had one eye on the mirror as you watched yourself gavotte.*
> *And all the girls dreamed that they'd be your partner*
> *They'd be your partner, and...*
>
> *You're so vain, you probably think this song is about you.*
> *You're so vain, I'll bet you think this song is about you.*

Don't you? Don't You?

A 'third person' lyric will employ the pronouns: he, she, it, him, her, his, hers, and its. 'Third person' is used for most narrative story telling. At first glance the 'third person' may seem less personal and may not possess the automatic bias and emotional charge of a first or second person telling, but it's the story you tell that matters, as much as how you tell it.

In practice, many songs will employ combinations of first, second and third person while telling their tale. Hal David's lyrics to the classic, 'Close to You', uses all three in its first couplet:

> *Why do birds, suddenly appear every time you are near?*
> *Just like me, they long to be close to you.*

It doesn't matter what approach you take, or what combination of perspectives you deploy. The point is, by simply being aware that each of these perspectives can put a different spin on your lyric, you can then exercise that much more control and choice over how your song evolves, and how it's likely to impact your listeners.

- **RHYME (& OTHER POETIC DEVICES)** – *Are you having fun playing with words?* There are a slew of poetic devices, rhyme being the most obvious one, which can be easily applied to song lyrics. Used properly, they're sure to enhance the listener's experience. If you're not using 'em, you gotta ask yourself – why not?

RHYME – You know what a rhyme is – two or more words, or parts of words, that sound alike: *moon, June, spoon, macaroon.* [NOTE: even Dylan rhymed *moon* with *spoon* in his song, 'I'll Be Your Baby Tonight'.]

I'm going to refrain from offering up pages and pages of examples of typical rhymes. It'd be a tedious waste of time, bore me to tears and probably put you to all to sleep. Like I just said, you know what a rhyme is. Instead I'm going to focus on some of the less familiar utilizations of rhyme, such as internal rhymes and false rhymes. (You're welcome.)

Usually, when we think of rhymes we mean the last syllable or two (or three) of a word at the end of a phrase. But rhymes can occur all over the place, and not just on the last syllable; it's just that when they do they're sometimes given different names.

For example, if a rhyme occurs between vowels in the middle of a lyric phrase, instead of at the end, it's often called assonance or an internal rhyme. Assonance refers to the repetition of a vowel sound within a phrase. Consonance refers to the repetition of a consonant sound within a phrase. They're both a kind of internal rhyme. Got that?

Here's my only problem: when I hear the word assonance, my admittedly still adolescent brain just hears the word *assonance* – yeah, I know, I'm an idiot. And as for the word consonance, what can I say? It's just so vague and nebulous sounding, it really bothers me for some reason. I'm not sure why. In any case, I can't in good conscience burden you with having to remember it; you have enough important stuff to remember in your complicated lives to have to worry about a pair of stupid words like assonance and consonance. So, for the purposes of this handbook and because I'm doing my best to avoid turning this slender treatise into a clumsily written, over-stuffed, half-assed (or half-assonanced), English Grammar primer, let's just call 'em internal rhymes - 'cause that's what they are.

INTERNAL RHYMES

Internal rhymes are rhymes that seem to occur almost inadvertently somewhere in the middle of a line, or even near the beginning - as opposed to the end of a line. Internal rhymes possess a subtle power by knitting a stanza together without being blatantly obvious about it. An internal rhyme serves to punctuate a lyrical phrase, without necessarily calling too much attention to itself, and thereby allowing the line to continue its flow.

Check out this profusion of internal rhymes by a fellow songwriter from the great state of New Jersey in the song, 'Blinded by the Light' [by the Boss, aka Bruce Springsteen]:

Madman drummers, bummers and Indians in the summer with a teenage diplomat.
In the dumps with the mumps as the adolescent pumps

his way into his hat.
With a boulder on my shoulder, feelin' kinda older, I
tripped the merry-go-round.
With this very unpleasing sneezing and wheezing, the
calliope crashed to the ground.
Some all-hot half-shot was headin' for the hot spot,
snappin' his fingers, clappin' his hands.
And some fleshpot mascot was tied into a lover's knot
with a whatnot in her hand.
And now young Scott with a slingshot finally found a
tender spot and throws his lover in the sand.
And some bloodshot forget-me-not whispers, "Daddy's
within earshot, save the buckshot, turn up the band".
And she was blinded by the light...

This song is so chock-full of lyrics, that spill out in a torrent with each verse, that it's not readily apparent just how many internal rhymes are actually contained in this lyric – until you look squarely at the printed text (like you're doing now). And then, it may come as a shock and surprise to discover how carefully and tightly crafted each of these couplets is. Not only are there internal rhymes within the couplets but there is internal rhyming between couplets. I'm convinced it has something to do with the petrochemical fumes exuding from thousands of cars on the New Jersey Turnpike. We'll never know. Whatever the cause, the result is a thrilling example of how internal rhymes can provide cohesion, texture and propulsion to a lyric. The words grab you by the ears, toss you in the backseat of a 1932 Ford 'Deuce' and send you cruising at breakneck speed, down the highway, by the Jersey shore.

> Springsteen reportedly claims to have written this song with a rhyming dictionary and is quoted as saying, *"The rhyming dictionary was on fire!"* Take note!

FALSE RHYMES

Most of rhymes in the Springsteen example, above, are what are sometimes referred to as 'true' rhymes, also called 'perfect' or 'full' or 'exact' rhymes. Rhymes like *hand, sand* and *band* or *round* and *ground* are considered 'true' or 'perfect' rhymes because their end sounds match exactly. Rhymes that don't match exactly are called 'false' rhymes.

So called, 'false' rhymes (also called 'close' or 'near' rhymes) hint at a rhyme without landing squarely on it. For example, if *love* and *dove* are considered perfect rhymes, *love* and *tough*, would be considered false or close rhymes. Other examples of false rhymes could include...

pickle and *wiggle*
plant and *land*
peace and *breeze*
often and *muffin*

There are some traditionalists that would be aghast at suggestion that those words rhyme. God bless 'em.

There's an expression that goes, *Close only counts in horseshoes and hand grenades.* I would have to add *'false' rhymes* to that adage. So called, 'false' rhymes count. There's nothing false about 'em.

Check out the rhymes, including false and internal rhymes that Eminem (Mr. Marshall Mathers) spits out in this excerpt from his song, 'Rhyme or Reason':

It's like handing a psycho a loaded handgun
Michelangelo with a paint gun in a tantrum
About to explode all over the canvas
Back with the Yoda of rap in a spasm
(Your music usually has them)
(But waned for the game your enthusiasm it hasn't)

Not content with a cascade of clever false and internal rhymes (notice the preponderance of 'o's and 'an's), Eminem pulls a triple between *spasm* and the last few words, *enthusiasm it hasn't* (and he manages this while remaining true to Yoda's typically fractured sentence structure – i.e. impressed with him, I am). His overt misogyny aside, Mr. Mathers deserves to copyright his own rhyming dictionary, because for damn sure you're not going find *tantrum* as a rhyme for *handgun* in the one sitting on your library shelf.

While we're on the subject of **rhyming dictionaries**, permit me to express my personal position on the supposed controversy regarding the use of rhyming dictionaries and other reference books. It's this:

THERE IS NO CONTRAVERSY! USE THEM!

Like the Boss, I'm a *huge* fan of rhyming dictionaries and all kinds of reference books, including dictionaries and thesauruses (I could have used thesauri, but I wanted to see if my spell checker would let me type thesauruses. Apparently, both are acceptable. Whew!).

Just to be absolutely clear, here, leaving no room for doubt, I would have to say, in no uncertain terms, that anyone that doesn't use some version of a rhyming dictionary or thesaurus – hardcopy, paperback or online - must be a certified dolt. NOTE: I actually just used an online thesaurus to come up with a synonym for someone of minimal intelligence, in an effort to avoid offending anyone that is actually mentally challenged, as opposed to the type of *flea-brain* that refuses to use a rhyming dictionary because they imagine, somehow, that it might be a form of cheating, or worse, uncool! (I did *not* require a thesaurus to come up with that insectual characterization. And, also, if you imagine yourself to be cooler than The Boss, well then, you truly are delusional! ;-)

Using a rhyming dictionary is not cheating, of course. Every accomplished songwriter worth their salt has at least one dog-eared copy of a rhyming dictionary, plus a conventional dictionary and thesaurus, close at hand. That's a fact.

If you don't have 'em – go out and buy 'em, today. Seriously, stop reading, get in your car, drive to the nearest book store and buy yourself at least one good rhyming dictionary, regular dictionary and thesaurus. O.K., the truth is, these days, you don't even have to buy one. If you have even the flimsiest of internet connections, you can find plenty of decent rhyming, thesaurus and dictionary websites online. Just type the word in question followed by either 'rhyme' or 'synonym' or 'define' into your browser and today's modern version of all these reference books will pop up on your screen.

There are also a whole new generation of songwriting apps and fully developed songwriting programs, that have come out in the last few years, that offer a suite of useful features including rhyming, alliteration, thesaurus, dictionary and idiomatic phrase modules, along with note-taking and audio recording features, all integrated into a comprehensive package. Check 'em out. Use whatever works for you.

Personally, I prefer my own well-worn hardcopies; easier to throw across the room at the cat when he is bothering me to get fed and I'm trying to get some work done (don't worry, I only fantasize about doing this. Besides, he's pretty quick.). In fact, I have several copies of each scattered around the house, so one is always within arm's reach, just in case the muse happens to strike. Reference books like rhyming dictionaries, dictionaries and thesauri (see?) are just as important to a songwriter as a hammer is to a carpenter, or a wrench is to a plumber, or a glass-cutter is to a cat-burglar, or... you get the idea.

But, remember this: as useful as all these reference books (or websites) are – and they are *extremely* useful, invaluable, in fact - don't expect to find *all* the answers to your lyric puzzles in them. It's still your job as a songwriter to come up with new and interesting and clever ways of combining words with notes in order to say what you want to say.

RHYME SCHEME – We see that rhymes can occur anywhere in a lyric phrase – at the end, beginning or middle. The pattern in which your rhymes occur is referred to as the rhyme scheme.

The purpose of this book is not to advise you what types of rhyme schemes to deploy, but merely to remind you of the many different kinds of rhyme schemes at your disposal.

Song lyrics are a kind of poetry – the main difference being that a song lyric is wedded to a melody and can do certain things a poem alone cannot. I'll address that curious coupling later on, but first I simply want to make the point that most of the same rules and non-rules of poetry apply. As far as rhyme schemes goes, it's mostly a matter of where you place your rhymes – where they land - or whether you even rhyme at all. Do your main rhymes occur at the end of lines 1 & 2 and also lines 3 & 4 [AABB]? Or do they occur at the end of lines 1 & 3 and also lines 2 & 4? [ABAB]. Or do your rhymes happen at the end of lines 1 & 4? And 2 & 3? And are you employing internal rhymes within those couplets? The combinations and variations are endless. I mean, seriously, if I started listed examples of different kinds of lyric rhyme schemes this book would weigh several tons and that would just be volume one in an ongoing series.

But just for the hell of it, here are a few more different types of rhyme schemes for your perusal, to help you get a sense of the enormous variety that exists.

Enjoy the first verse of 'Up the Junction' [by Squeeze: Chris Difford, Glen Tilbrook and Christopher Henry]

> *I never thought it would happen*
> *With me and the girl from Clapham*
> *Out on the windy common*
> *That night I ain't forgotten*
> *When she dealt out the rations*
> *With some or other passions*
> *I said "you are a lady"*
> *"Perhaps" she said. "I may be"*

It goes on like that, couplet after couplet, for the rest of the song, a new rhyme every couplet; snappy, clever, charming, and at the same time, very, very real. Gotta love Squeeze.

And here are two verses from the classic gem, 'Will You Love Me Tomorrow' [by Carole King and Gerry Goffin]

> *Tonight you're mine completely*
> *You give your love so sweetly*
> *Tonight the light of love is in your eyes*
> *But will you love me tomorrow?*

> *Is this a lasting treasure*
> *Or just a moment's pleasure*
> *Can I believe the magic of your sighs*
> *Will you still love me tomorrow?*

Notice that in the first verse, the end of the third line appears to have no rhyme at all. That is until you get to the same spot (third line) in the second verse, where lo' and behold – a rhyming couplet – *eyes* and *sighs* – connect with each other, an entire verse apart

ABSENCE OF RHYME

You don't hear it that often in a typical pop or country song, but every now and then a song will use the temporary *absence* of rhyme (or implied absence) to suggest a feeling of instability or impermanence, or just to make us perk up our ears and listen because we've been conditioned to hear something happen which didn't. And often, the lack of an anticipated rhyme can lend a conversational tone to a lyric.

Here's the last verse and chorus of Jakob Dylan's (The Wallflowers), very tasty, 'One Headlight':

Well this place is old
It feels just like a beat up truck
I turn the engine, but the engine doesn't turn
Well it smells of cheap wine & cigarettes
This place is always such a mess
Sometimes I think I'd like to watch it burn
I'm so alone, and I feel just like somebody else
Man, I ain't changed, but I know I ain't the same
But somewhere here in between the city walls of dyin'
dreams.
I think her death it must be killin' me

Hey, come on try a little
Nothing is forever
There's got to be something better than
In the middle
But me & Cinderella
We put it all together
We can drive it home
With one headlight

The chorus has a few vaguely false internal rhymes between *little* and *middle* and also *forever*, *better*, *Cinderella* and *together* and then ends with *one headlight,* which for all practical purposes has no rhyme at all (although you could argue a slight bit of assonance... oops, I meant *internal* rhyme with the word *drive*).

But, if you examine the verse, other than the obvious rhyme between *turn* and *burn*, there are only a few stray internal rhymes and a last line, *must be killin' me,* that purposefully ends with no corresponding rhyme in sight. The effect of that last non-rhyming line is that it feels as if the verse hasn't ended yet, as if there's still something yet to come - which turns out to be a terrific way of setting of the catchy chorus that follows.

Interestingly, this absence of rhyme doesn't happen in the preceding two verses, which have a more conventional rhyme scheme. And curiously, there's also a long-distance rhyme (not shown above) between the last word of the first line of the second verse - *She said it's cold* - and the last word of the first line of this third verse - *...this place is old.* So, I'm not saying that Jakob has thrown rhymes and rhyme scheme completely out the window, only that rather than rhyme compulsively, he's being selective about it; he's leaving rhymes out when they don't serve his immediate purpose, and the choice results in an appealingly loose, narrative quality to the lyric. Which is pretty cool!

Here's a rhyme scheme example from one of my tunes, 'Love is Not Enough', which starts off at a moderately slow tempo with a lyric that delays its rhymes for so long that you almost never expect them to arrive at all, and when they finally do arrive, they include two false, internal rhymes and an extremely loose, stop-and-start phrasing, the cumulative effect of which results in a conversational lyric that almost seems spoken rather than sung.

> *If I've managed to learn anything at all from what we've done,*
> *It's that even though it fills the cracks and crevices, and mends the tattered souls,*
> *Still we're each other's nemesis, and two halves do not always make a whole.*
> *And though you know I've often heard it said we're made of sterner stuff.*
> *Love is not enough. Love is not enough.*

The fact that there's not really a stand-along chorus – the song is all 'verse' with a simple repeated tag-line, *'Love is not enough',* further reinforces the conversational quality of the lyric.

All these rhyming elements – rhyme, non-rhyme, false rhyme, internal rhyme - work together, as in the examples above, to provide texture, character and a kind of lyric-harmony to a song. So, give some occasional thought to not just *how*, but also *where* you rhyme – or don't.

THOSE OTHER POETIC DEVICES

We've already talked about rhyme, which is fundamental to almost every song lyric. And we've touched on internal rhymes and false (or close) rhymes. But how about trying your hand at some of these other cool poetic device?: simile, metaphor, alliteration, repetition, contrast, hyperbole, personification… All forms of writing use them sometimes. Poetry uses them all the time. Lyrics - a kind of poetry wedded to a melody – uses them a lot. The odds are you're already using them yourself, whether you're aware of it or not. Either way, let's see what each of these devices has to offer a songwriter.

SIMILE & METAPHOR

Simile and Metaphor are pretty much the same, with one small difference. They're both devices that a writer uses to compare one thing to another. The only difference is that if you compare things using the words 'like' or 'as' it's called a simile; if you compare things *without* using the words 'like' or 'as' it's called a metaphor. We recognize similes and metaphors as 'figures of speech'.

SIMILES

Here are some similes (they compare things using 'like' or 'as' or 'than'):

> They made love *like* rabbits
> He stands tall *as* a house.
> She sings as sweetly *as* a bird.
> He lived *like* a king.
> It's more fun *than* a barrel of monkeys.

So if, like Madonna, you feel, '*like* a virgin', you're using a simile (uses the word 'like') to compare yourself to an innocent, untouched virgin.

Same as when Dylan sings, you're 'on your own, *like* a rolling stone'. (uses the word 'like') He's comparing the feeling of being on your own to the careening, out-of-control, rootlessness of a rolling stone.

And, if 'you're cold *as* ice' as in the Foreigner lyric by Mick Jones and Lou Gramm, that's also a simile (uses the word 'as') You're not actually that cold, but they're suggesting, with a simile, that emotionally you are the opposite of warm, in fact you're below freezing.

Just as Jethro Tull's Ian Anderson knows how it feels to be 'thick *as* a brick'. (uses the word 'as') He's using a metaphor to describe someone as stubbornly dumb, as thick, dense and difficult to move as a brick.

Here's one of my favorite song simile's from Paul Simon's 'Graceland':

'The Mississippi Delta was shining *like* a National guitar...'

If you've ever seen the gleaming steel resonator top of a National guitar, you'll appreciate just how perfect that simile is; and even if you haven't, the simile still paints a vivid picture of that river delta in your mind.

And check out this sweet bundle of simile's in Redman's 'Green Island':

My style's rugged *like* Timberland
When I clock lyric then women give me more love *than* Wimbledon
My style flow local *like* New Jersey transit
And I can't stand it.

All of the above 'like' or 'as' or 'than' comparisons are called similes.

METAPHORS

Now if you make a comparison *without* using the words 'like' or 'as' or 'than', you're using a metaphor. Here are some examples:

This room is a pigsty.
She has a bubby personality.
It's raining cats and dogs.
She stared at me with daggers in her eyes.

So, in her song, 'Rolling in the Dark', when Adele sings, *'There's a fire starting in my heart'*, I suspect she's not actually combusting and she doesn't have indigestion. She's using a metaphor to describe the fiery hot emotions she's feeling deep in her chest.

And when Elton John sings Bernie Taupin's lyrics to Tiny Dancer, describing her as having a *'pirate smile'*, he knows she's not really a pirate, but he's comparing her devilish expression to that of a pirate's, with a metaphor.

And when Chrissie Hyndes of the Pretenders sings about being *'back on the chain gang'*, she's not really standing out in the hot sun, pickax in hand, working on a chain gang, instead she's more than likely using a metaphor to describe the kind of a virtual imprisonment she and her loved one are forced into by economic necessity and the vicissitudes of life.

In Neil Young's song, 'Heart of Gold', he sings about being a miner for a heart of gold. He's making a comparison between an actual miner, down in the underground mines, looking for a valuable mineral and someone searching for a soul-mate with a good heart. Consider the following line:

I've been a miner for a heart of gold

Which is followed later by the following lines:

I've been in my mind, it's such a fine line
That keeps me searching for a heart of gold.

He's underscoring the metaphor with a pun that suggests a connection between the word 'mind' and the word 'mine'. He's a miner working the *mine*, and the *mind*, in his search for a heart of gold.

Lily Allen delivers up a boxing metaphor in her song, 'Sheezus', in which she describes her re-entry into a cut-throat music business, after a long hiatus, by comparing it to the perils of stepping into a boxing ring for a knock-'em down, drag-'em out fight.

> *Lace up my gloves, I'm going in.*
> *Don't let my kids watch me when I get in the ring*
> *I'll take the hits, roll with the punches*
> *I'll get back up, it's not as if I've never done this.*

Lily's lyrics are always clever, she's not shy about using a deft false rhyme (*punches / done this*), and like Neil, she manages to slip in a subtle pun to reinforce her 'boxing = record-biz' metaphor when she sings the line, 'I'll take the *hits*'.

In my song, 'Little Black Cloud', the metaphor is both obvious and apt, in this instance describing a fair lass who's gone through some difficult times, and is still grappling with trying to shake a vague sense of impending doom:

> *There's a little black cloud hanging over her head.*
> *No one can count the tears she's shed.*
> *There's a little black cloud that follows her around.*
> *But I'm gonna keep her safe and sound. Safe and*
> *sound.*

In the last few three metaphor examples - 'Heart of Gold', 'Sheezus' and 'Little Black Cloud' - the same metaphor was being used thematically, in slightly different, but related ways, throughout the songs. When similar metaphors are used repeatedly in proximity to each other, they're referred to as an 'extended metaphor'. There's no good reason for you to know this. It was kind of obvious without me having to put a label to it. I'm not even sure why I bothered mentioning it. So sue me.

Just one thing though, if you do consider taking me to court remember, you can't get blood from a stone. You'd just be beating your head against the wall, nailing Jello to a tree, trying to get the toothpaste back into the tube.

It won't be a walk in the park, that's for sure!

HYPERBOLE

Now, in the previous example I just used – the chorus of Little Black Cloud – I wrote the line:

No one can count the tears she's shed.

Now, technically, that's not exactly true. If one were determined and patient it would probably be possible to come up with a formula based on crying duration, tear volume and tear-drops per ounce over time that would enable you to at least provide a ball park estimate of just how many tears she's shed. That formula might look something like this:

C (crying) x D (duration) x V (volume) / TDpoz (TearDrops-peronce) = TSS (Tears She's Shed)

O.K., I'm just messing with you.

[Remember, always use your own judgement, you've got a brain, trust your instincts and don't take anything I (or they) say as gospel.]

But, the point I *was* trying to make is that a trained ophthalmologist could probably come up with a reasonable estimate for how many tears she's shed – give or take a few thousand tears.

So, you *could* argue that the line is a slight exaggeration.

The term 'hyperbole' refers to the use of exaggeration to emphasize an idea. It's not meant to be taken literally.

So, when you hear Marvin Gaye and Tammi Terrell sing the chorus to the song, 'Ain't No Mountain High Enough' [by Nickolas Ashford & Valerie Simpson]…

Ain't no mountain high enough. Oh baby there
ain't no mountain high enough,
Ain't no valley low enough,
Ain't no river wide enough
To keep me from getting to you babe

In point of fact, there are probably a few very tall mountains (Mt. Everest? Mt McKinley? K2?) that would, indeed, be high enough to keep them from getting to each other. And no doubt there are a few treacherous rivers in this world that would make it extremely difficult, if not impossible, for either of them to cross. Valleys? I'm not so sure. (Death Valley?) In any case, the lyric is using exaggeration to emphasize how much they love each other. That's hyperbole. [note: hyperbole can also function as a metaphor or a simile, if two ideas are being compared to each other.]

Figures of speech like…

I'm so hungry I could eat a horse.
These shoes are killing me.
This day will never end.
I've told you a million times…

… are all examples of hyperbole.

Songs like…

Eight Days a Week [Lennon & McCartney]
Fly Me to The Moon [by Bart Howard]
Cry Me a River [by Arthur Hamilton]
I've Been Everywhere [by Geoff Mack]
Eight Miles High [by Gene Clark, Roger McGuinn and David Crosby]

… are using hyperbole.

When Marc Cohn, sings in 'Walking In Memphis', that he, '...was walking with my feet ten feet off of Beale', he's using hyperbole.

And when Sting sang, 'Every breath you take, every move you make... I'll be watching you.', let's face it, he may be a deranged, monomaniacal stalker, but still, he's exaggerating – just a bit.

Do you recall the songs I referenced earlier talking about TONE, ATTITUDE and PERSONA?: 'Hoochie Coochie Man', 'Bad to the Bone' and 'Wonder'. All three used exaggeration to make their point. Hyperbolic all the way!

Hyperbole. Use it correctly, and I guarantee your songs will improve *one thousand percent!* O.K. that may have been a touch hyperbolic. But you get the idea, right?

PERSONIFICATION

Personification is another one of those fun devices that lets you playfully distort reality in order to express yourself. Personification is when you attribute human characteristics to something nonhuman (like an animal or inanimate object, like say a sofa or a piano.)

Whenever your heart aches, or your soul hungers, or the sun kisses your cheek, or the moon winks, or the words seem to leap off the page, you're witnessing personification.

If the mosquitoes in your yard declare war, or your cat eyes you suspiciously, or your neighbor's dog waltzes right into your living room… it might be time to move. Because you've got a serious case of personification.

When Jimi Hendrix sings, 'The Wind Cries Mary', that's personification.

And when The Captain and Tennille or America sing about 'Muskrat Love' [by Willis Alan Ramsey], personification is afoot. [actually, this is anthropomorphism, but we're just splitting hares here, and the difference is so slight that we could argue about it 'til the cows come home.]

Tom Waits employs personification to great effect when he mumbles the lyrics to his song, 'The Piano Has Been Drinking (Not Me)'

> *The piano has been drinking, my necktie is asleep*
> *And the combo went back to New York, the jukebox has*
> *to take a leak.*
> *And the carpet needs a haircut, and the spotlight looks*
> *like a prison break.*
> *And the telephone's out of cigarettes, and the balcony is*
> *on the make.*
> *And the piano has been drinking, the piano has been*

drinking...

Stubbornly denying his own inebriated state, Tom lays the blame on the nearest available scapegoats, who, at least in this case, are unable to defend themselves.

The amazing songwriter, comedian and surrealist, Boothby Graffoe, employs personification, or some strange hybrid version of it, in his hilarious and poignant, 'Poor Umbrella Head Boy':

She'll only take him out when it's raining
She won't take him out when the sun's in the sky
She'll only take him out when it's raining
Poor umbrella head boy

In my song, Rocking Chair (It's Gonna Be All Right), I make extensive use of personification by attributing human characteristics to all the furniture and appliances in my apartment.

In this song, the inanimate inhabitants of my one-room, rent-controlled apartment, begin offering me all sorts of sage advice (which might have served me well, if I'd actually taken it) in an attempt to shake me out of a temporary funk. Note that once I decided to adopt personification as the framework for this song, I made specific choices about who was saying what, based on their individual attributes, as I'll explain below. Here's the song:

Rocking Chair (It's Gonna Be All Right)

"Well, well," said the rocking chair.
"It's been a while since I've seen such stark despair."
"Who told you like was fair?"
"Woa, woa," said the radio,
"Sit, there are some things you ought to know"
"There is little you can do to stop the pain
and it's gonna happen time and time again,
but just remember even though it sounds insane,
it's impossible to ever love somebody in vain."

All right. It's gonna be all right.
It's gonna be all right. It's gonna be all right.

"No, no," said the balcony, "If it's pity you want don't come to me."
"No, nothing comes for free."
"Yes, yes," said the coffee cup,
"maybe now is the time to act grown up."
"If you feel like your world is crashing in,
simply dial up your nearest kith or kin."
"If you open up and let them in,
you'll discover that you'll probably make it through once again."

All right. It's gonna be all right…

"Hey, hey," said the table top, "don't be making like you're anything you're not."
"Make do with what you've got".
"Don't forget," said the cuckoo clock,
"any parts you need we've got in stock."
"Take a look at the place you call your home.
You're reflected in all the things you own.
And the seeds of reason you have sown,
they're a measure of a part of you that's already grown."

All right. It's gonna be all right.
It's gonna be all right. It's gonna be all right.

Here's the key to explaining what characteristics each inanimate object represents and why they offer the advice they do:

The *Rocking Chair* is a place you sit to relax and be comforted, but even though the Rocking Chair is the first object in the house to recognize that need, it's not especially comforting, rather it challenges me to be realistic about the situation: *'Who told you, life was fair?'.* Which is, in a way, its own kind of comfort, though not necessarily the comfort I was looking for.

The *Radio* is a natural announcer and broadcaster of useful messages and so gets right to the point. *"There is little you can do to stop the pain and it's gonna happen time and time again… (but) it's gonna be all right."*

The *Balcony* - a place where really desperate people go to

jump - is refusing to feel sorry for my plight - , *"If it's pity you want don't come to me."* - and admonishing me not to feel sorry for myself.

I view the *Coffee Cup* as a badge of adult-hood (most kids I know don't start their day with a warm cuppa java). In that spirit, it's helpfully offering this encouraging advice: *"maybe now is the time to act grown up."*

The *Table Top* represents surface appearances rather than substance - what *seems* to be going on rather than what's really going on. In other words, don't be in denial, don't kid yourself about who you are - *"don't be making like you're anything you're not."* – Be honest with yourself about what you bring to the table (so to speak): "Make do with what you've got".

And, finally, the *Cuckoo Clock*, which for me represents the crazy, insane and transformative power of creativity and imagination – the secret ingredient to survival. *"Don't forget,"* said the cuckoo clock, *"any parts you need we've got in stock."* Or, in other words, if you find yourself stuck in a jam, or serious depression, with no apparent solution, don't despair. Even if you don't thing you have any options available to you, as a very last resort you can always use your imagination to come up with a creative solution to rescue you from your funk.

At least, that's what I think the Cuckoo Clock was saying. I never knew for sure. I mean, it was a talking Cuckoo Clock, who knows what it was thinking?

I only have a vague recollection of what sparked the initial idea for this song – I know I worked out the chord progressions improvising on a hotel lobby piano, somewhere in Pittsburgh, PA. I do recall that as soon as I came up with the very first lyric line, I already had a roadmap for completing it.

As I've said before – and will say again - I always try to figure out what my song is about, the sooner the better. That's your roadmap. It provides you with a goal and a strategy for getting there. I then went about generating lists of couplets in which inanimate objects in my apartment offered unsolicited advice. I consciously recall asking myself, 'what type of advice would each different object be likely to provide, based on their innate characteristics?'. In other words, I interrogated my existing material, in order to figure out what new material might come next. I arranged the couplets in an order that made some kind of whimsical sense.

Even when dealing with talking furniture you strive to impose some kind of internal logic on the proceedings. And it doesn't require much in-depth analysis to conclude that I was really having the entire conversation with myself, seeing as, *'you're reflected in all the things you own.'* Be that as it may, even after all these years, it still seems like pretty good advice.

ALLITERATION

Alliteration is when you string together a bunch of words that all begin with the same consonant. As kids we first become familiar with alliteration in 'tongue-twisters':

Peter Piper picked a peck of pickled peppers.
She sells seashells down by the seashore

And once you start listening, you'll hear plenty of examples in all kinds of songs.

In his song, 'Let it Be', when you hear Paul McCartney sing, *'whisper words of wisdom, let it be.'*, that's alliteration.

When Elvis Costello sings in his song, 'Veronica' about, *'...all the lips that he licks.'*, that's alliteration.

Same with Lori Lieberman's song, 'Killing Me Softly': *'I felt all flushed with fever, embarrassed by the crowd...'* – alliteration.

And consider this example by Tupac in his song, 'If I Die 2nite': *'They say pussy and paper is poetry, power and pistols, picturin' pitiful punk...'*

You get the idea.

Alliteration can help a lyric to flow and, at the same time, give it a type of cohesion, causing the words to nicely mesh. Alliteration can add a kind of musical, sing-song quality to a line of text. And its repetitive use of a consonant can inject an almost hypnotic quality into a song lyric, quietly seducing the listener with its rolling rhythms.

In my song, 'Where Have All the Angels Flown?', I intentionally searched for lines that were rich with alliteration. I did this, in part, to offset the grim story I was telling.

> *Sprawling spired skylines, sparkle in the night*
> *Sprinkling angel dust on everything in sight.*
> *In the shadows far below, nestled deep within,*
> *Lies a cardboard shanty town shaking in the wind.*

One of my favorite examples of alliteration can be heard in Stephen Stills, 'Helplessly Hoping' from his Crosby, Stills, Nash and Young days. Check out the first and second lines of these verses:

> *Helplessly hoping her harlequin hovers nearby, awaiting a word.*
> *Gasping at glimpses of gentle true spirit he runs, wishing he could fly. Only to trip at the sound of goodbye.*

> *Wordlessly watching he waits by the window and wonders at the empty place inside.*
> *Heartlessly helping himself to her bad dreams he worries, did he hear a good-bye? Or even hello?*

Alliteration can be a powerful tool in your songwriting tool chest, but one note of caution: too much alliteration can sometimes run the risk of drawing too much attention to itself – and *away* from the meaning of the lyric. As with all of these poetic devices, you need to find the right balance for the task at hand.

REPETITION (and its opposite – SPACE)

Alliteration is closely related to rhyme in that they both involve the repetition of a sound. And if you think about it, it's no accident that the words rhyme and rhythm share a common derivation. They're closely related in that they both involve repeating patterns. And despite being obtuse about a lot of stuff in our lives, one thing our brains are especially good at is pattern recognition. We respond to patterns – rhythmic, musical and lyrical patterns - automatically and viscerally.

There are all sorts of ways to apply repetition in a song – to the lyrics, to the music or, because they're usually inextricably entwined, to both.

The most basic repetition in a song is the return of the chorus. Every time a chorus repeats, we experience a sense of satisfaction at its familiarity – we've recognized its pattern. Its lyrical meaning and its musical identity is reinforced and our minds are primed to anticipate its return. The same thing happens, but more quickly and on a smaller scale, with single words and short phrases.

There's an hypnotic power in repeating a single lyric or phrase. It's a way to reinforce and underline an idea. In its simplest terms it's a sure-fire way to grab your ear's attention. Think of all the pop songs that start out by repeating the first word of the hook:

> *Sugar, Sugar*
> *Baby, Baby*, Don't Get Hooked on Me
> *Bye, Bye Love*
> *Hey, Hey, We're the Monkees*
> *Hey (Hey), You (You) Get Off of My Cloud*
> *Louie, Louie*
> (credits listed in same order as above song titles)

> [by Jeff Barry and Andy Kim sung by the Archies]
> [by Mac Davis]
> [by Felice and Boudleaux Bryant / sung by the Everly Brothers]
> [by Tommy Boyce and Bobby Hart / sung by the Monkees]
> [by Mick Jagger and Keith Richards / Rolling Stones]
> [by Richard Berry / sung by The Kingsmen]

Whole phrases can reap the same benefits of repetition, including this ultimate classic:

She Loves You, Yeah, Yeah, Yeah,
She Loves You, Yeah, Yeah, Yeah,
She Loves You, Yeah, Yeah, Yeah.

['She Loves You' by Lennon & McCartney]

One of the important reasons the lyric repetitions in 'She Loves You' works so well (aside from the fact that it's the friggin' Beatles, for goodness sakes!) is that even as the lyrical phrase repeats exactly, the music underneath it changes with each repetition of the lyric, providing you the satisfaction of familiar material combined with the excitement of new material – all at the same time.

This underscores the main difference between poetry and lyrics, the simple fact that a lyric, because it's wedded to music, can do things a poem alone cannot. For example...

Consider another classic lyric from the song, 'Me and Mrs. Jones' by Kenny Gamble, Leon Huff and Cary 'Hippy' Gilbert performed originally by Billy Paul, a powerful emotive tune about a clandestine affair. There's an amazing section in this song which serves as a pickup to the actual chorus. The basic lyric to this pickup is simply, *Me and Mrs. Jones*, but making exquisite use of repetition it's sung like this:

Me, ee, aa, and Mrs., Mrs. Jones, Mrs. Jones, Mrs. Jones, Mrs. Jones... We've got a thing going on.

You'll definitely have to listen to this online to fully appreciate what's happening. But I'll try to break it down for you, as best I can.

First, the words *me* and *and* are split in half, the words elongated and each syllable sung with an accented pulse, so that the 'e' in *me* is repeated twice and the 'a' in *and* is repeated twice. Next, the word *Mrs.* is repeated twice. Finally the words *Mrs. Jones* are repeated four times.

All this accelerating repetition builds up to a stunning, climactic chorus.

On some level it's meaningless to analyze a song this good or to try and figure out how it got that way. Some kind of magic happened and this song was the result. But for the purposes of this book, I'm willing to play the fool and simply point out that the mysterious power of repetition definitely plays some small part in it.

Continuing in this vein, permit me to foolishly offer one more example of how repetition can be deployed, illustrated by my song, Lydia.

The first verse of Lydia goes...

> *Lydia keeps my toothbrush in her apartment and she never complains. Well hardly ever. But then jokingly she says,*
> *"Boy, it's been so long since I've held you, I nearly gave you up for dead. I nearly gave you up for dead. I nearly gave you up for dead.*

The phrase, '*I nearly gave you up for dead*' is repeated three times in a row but curiously, that fact is not readily apparent to most listeners. I think the reason for that is that with each repetition of the phrase the underlying harmony, as well as the vocal delivery, changes ever so slightly, making each phrase seem distinct and imparting an evolving tone and new meaning to each line. The first occurrence of the line can seem almost joking. The second occurrence seems slightly less joking, almost wistful. And finally the third occurrence is not joking at all, in fact, it's dead serious.

Meanwhile, something quite the opposite happens in the third verse of Lydia. Let me explain...

We've just touched on the idea that our ability to recognize repeating patterns in songs, primes us to then anticipate a repeat of those same patterns. It's inexplicably satisfying when they return. But what if they don't? What happens when you set up a repeating pattern, train the listener to expect the pattern to return again and again, but *instead* you do something entirely different – you stray from that familiar pattern. Well, that's when things get interesting. That's when, if you do it right, you can get your listener to suddenly sit up, mid-song, and take notice, and ask, 'Hey, what's going on here? Maybe I need to pay a little more attention to this bit, to see if I can understand better.'

You're doing a feint. A little sleight of hand. You're suggesting one musical direction to your listener but then, when they least expect it, you drag (or gently nudge them) somewhere else.

This is essentially what happens in the last verse of Lydia.

> *I sleep with a woman who thinks I'm a child. Well, maybe I am. No, that wouldn't surprise anyone. I suspect that much is true.*
> *But, Lydia, if you only knew how much I love you.*
> *[long lyric pause]........ Did you know that I love you?*
> *It's the best that I can do.*

From the beginning of the song, I'm singing a lyric over every single measure in both the verses and the choruses. But suddenly in the last verse, I stop. The pattern is interrupted. The music continues, but in a section of the verse where your ear has been conditioned, over and over again, to hear a lyrical phrase, a familiar rhythmic patter of words, at that particular part of the verse, there is .... a huge gap! A space. A lyric is missing.

There is a predictable reaction to that gap, which is that the listener inevitably, if unconsciously, focuses their attention on whatever happens next. They're still waiting for that other shoe to drop. They know something's coming, but they don't know what or when, so they lean in with anticipation to what you're about to say. And when that follow-up lyric finally arrives, you can bet they'll hear it. And that's the point. That gap. That break in the lyrical pattern. That space serves to emphasize the next line, *'Did you know that I love you?',* which just happens to be the whole point of the song.

We're talking about two opposing but related properties here - repetition and space. Repetition is how we tend to organize our content, our patterns. Space is one way of interrupting or diverging from those patterns. We could also have simply altered the pattern in some other way, but in this example, space – the lack of repetition - provides the crucial ingredient - contrast.

CONTRAST

Contrast keeps things interesting. It also highlights and differentiates what happens right next to it. Contrast is a fundamental part of any work of art. It gives form and shape to a piece.

In paintings and photographs, bright foreground objects are rendered more vivid by dark backgrounds. In dance, slow, sensuous movements stand out distinctly from quick, frantic ones. Contrast. In drama, a sudden burst of violence is more striking when committed by a previously calm and placid character. Contrast.

Contrast deals in opposites and difference: hard or soft, loud or quiet, rough or smooth, fast or slow, tight or loose. In songs, we use contrast all the time to define and differentiate sections of a song. The most familiar utilization of contrast is the discernable difference between a song's verses and its choruses. They serve different functions. They have different attributes. They stand in stark contrast to each other.

Consider the classic Doors tune, 'Light My Fire' [by Ray Manzarek, Robby Krieger and Jim Morrison].

The time to hesitate is through
No time to wallow in the mire
Try now we can only lose
And our love become a funeral pyre

Come on baby, light my fire
Come on baby, light my fire
Try to set the night on fire, yeah

The verse and chorus are not only in different keys (verse in Am; chorus in D) but they're in different modes (minor vs major). The contrast between the minor verses and the major choruses has a dramatic impact on the emotional content of the song, almost regardless of the lyrical content. The minor key verses are dark, sensuous, filled with angst and almost threatening. By contrast, the major key choruses are exuberant, confident, assured and approaching celebratory.

Yeah, I know it seems odd doing a contrast breakdown of the Doors. Does it really make sense to offer this kind of clinical analysis of the raw, combustible work of what's arguably America's greatest rock band?

Maybe not. But, hey, I just did.

TENSION & RELEASE

Another important aspect of contrast can be seen in the idea of 'tension and release'. Again, we're talking about ways to keep things interesting by imparting drama and movement to a song, and this applies to both music and lyrics. In terms of music, certain chords and chord progressions possess an innate quality of tension and release.

For example, in most situations, a dominant chord (a major chord with a 7th in it, like G7, C7, E7 etc...) will tend to naturally resolve to its tonic (G7 to C; C7 to F; E7 to A) – tension and release. Same thing with diminished chords and II, V progressions. Eventually, these chords and chord progressions seek some type of musical resolution. And we can all hear this, even if we're not technically aware of the harmonic theory behind it.

And without delving too deeply here into music theory and harmony, the point is that tension and release is a natural consequence of how chords move from one to another. As you learn to be able to recognize those kinds of progressions, you'll be better able to control and direct them to suit your needs.

One way to view this is to think of tension as the part of a song (the verse, for example) in which you take your listener on a journey, during which they're not exactly sure where they're going to wind up. You don't want to reveal everything up front – that's how you keep them engaged. They're trusting, or at least hoping, that you'll lead them safely to a pleasing destination.

When you finally do deliver them to a satisfying resolution (the tonic or the chorus, for example), you've provided them with a sense of release and relief. This concept of tension and release can occur on a macro scale between sections of a song or on a micro-scale, within a measure, or even between two notes or two chords. It's a type of contrast and it's all part of taking your listener on an interesting ride.

Tension and release happens in lyrics as well as in the music, and usually in both the lyrics and the music together.

When Billy Joel sings, 'We Didn't Start the Fire', the machine-gun-fire verses build with increasing anxiety and tension, culminating in a burning crescendo and sense of release, upon arriving at the chorus.

Verse

Einstein, James Dean, Brooklyn's got a winning team
Davy Crockett, Peter Pan, Elvis Presley, Disneyland
Bardot, Budapest, Alabama, Krushchev
Princess Grace, "Peyton Place", trouble in the Suez

Chorus

We didn't start the fire…

Tension and release are what Billy used to turn what might have otherwise been a mundane American History lesson into a thrilling piece of rock & roll.

DYNAMICS

Another instance of contrast – this time between loud and soft. It might happen between a verse and a chorus or between two words. A song without dynamics is gonna have a tough time keeping the attention of the listener. Done right, dynamics can keep your listener on the edge of their seat; you know, assuming they're actually sitting down, which in the next few examples they're most definitely not.

Think of Kurt Cobain's 'Smells Like Teen Spirit', or Billy

Corgan's 'Bullet with Butterfly Wings' or almost any alt-rock composition of the 80's and 90's. One feature these songs all have in common is a dramatically stark contrast between the dynamics of the verses vs the choruses. And this dynamic contrast is not just to do with volume; just as importantly it has to do with the attitude of the vocal and instrumental delivery. And while this issue of dynamics may seem to veer into the area of instrumental arrangement, audio mixing and performance, the genesis of it all is the structure of the song itself.

- **Lyrical Fit** (phrasing) – *Does your lyric fit tightly to your melody or does it flow loosely like casually spoken dialogue?* Some lyrics, especially in pop songs, fit tightly to a melody, landing squarely on the beat and locked rigidly into the rhythmic phrasing of each note in the melody. By contrast, some lyrics do just the opposite – they flow irregularly across and around the beat, stretching and bending the melodic phrasing and imparting a feeling of spoken dialogue.

In terms of a super-tight lyrical fit, think Taylor Swift's 'Shake it Off'. The lyric on both the verses and the infectious chorus fits tightly to a rigid melody, which itself is tied to a mechanically straight, even beat.

> *Cause the players gonna play, play, play, play, play and the Haters gonna hate, hate, hate, hate, hate…*

Terrific tune. It's inspired, catchy, musical and funny as hell (and the video is hilarious!). And even within its tight, rigid lyrical structure there's plenty of interesting stuff going on – nifty anticipations, emphasis on off-beats, infectious repetitions, strong melody. There's an almost maniacal consistency to its tight structure. And as such it's a perfect example of a pop song with a tight lyrical fit.

Now, by comparison, consider an example from the other end of the 'tight to loose lyric' spectrum: Joni Mitchell's 'A Case of You'

> *Just before our love got lost you said,*
> *"I am as constant as a northern star."*
> *And I said, "Constantly in the darkness, Where's that at?*
> *If you want me I'll be in the bar."*

Joni's lyric dances and skates all over, across and around the beat, dragging the melody along with it. It's almost as if she's purposefully ignoring the songs internal rhythmic pulse, but of course, she's not; she's relying on it as a kind of tether from which she's free to float above the beat, until the end of her lyrical phrase.

The effect is to make it appear as if the singer is engaged in a spoken conversation, which is exactly, in fact, what the lyric portrays - dialogue clearly punctuated as such. She could have sung the same lyrics tightly to a the beat, but phrasing it as loosely as she does, she manages to evoke the breathing, organic flow and pacing of spoken dialogue.

One interesting side effect of this loose phrasing is that it tends to de-emphasize what would otherwise be a very square rhyme between *star* and *bar.* Instead, because those rhymes don't land squarely on the beat, they almost sound like internal rhymes, a fact that is reinforced by the inclusion of the word, *darkness,* which actually *is* an internal rhyme. The end result is that at first listen, it's not immediately apparent that there are any rhyming couplets at all, except the whole verse fits perfectly together and flows naturally into the subsequent chorus.

This type of loose phrasing is more characteristic of jazz and some folk than of most pop, although you can find examples in pop and other idioms, like country, as well.

Whether your lyrical fit is tight as a drum or loose as a goose, it's just one more choice you get to make while crafting your songs.

Here are two more examples of both approaches – tight and loose – illustrated by two of my own tunes, 'McDonald's Girl' (tight fit) and Sandy (loose fit and tight fit):

> *I am in love with the McDonald's Girl*
> *She has the smile of innocence oh so tender and warm*
> *I am in love with the McDonald's Girl*
> *She is an angel in a polyester uniform*

Every single syllable of every word is tied tightly to an eighth note, and sung squarely on the beat. This holds true throughout the song, for the verses as well as the choruses.

By way of contrast, here's a verse from 'Sandy' (loose fit):

I fumble in my pockets for the keys to your fickle heart.
I drop them on the ground and then surprise, surprise you
pick 'em up.
So I stand in the doorway wearing my patented foolish grin.
'til finally you take pity on my poor soul and you let me in.
The time has come. Soon the ramparts will be overrun

Instead of being tied tightly to the beat, the phrasing in this verse is very loose; these lyrics almost seem to float independent of the underlying beat. That's not entirely true; each phrase has to begin and end within a rhythmic window defined by the harmonic progression, but as long as the delivery of that line fits within that time-frame, the singer has tremendous leeway as to how they can phrase the lyric and melody. It's an extremely loose lyrical fit.

As it happens, in the case of the song, 'Sandy', I made a conscious decision to shift from that loose fit to a tight lyrical fit within the same song, when the chorus finally arrives:

Sandy, won't you ever make up your mind?
The love you're trying so hard to find
Is standing right in front of you…

Just like the lyrics in McDonald's Girl, this chorus ties each syllable of each word tightly to the underlying beat. The loose phrasing of the verse is gone, replaced by a rigid, lyric and melody which is wedded tightly to the rhythm.

Why did I decide to make this shift? Something we talked about earlier - contrast. I purposefully strove to impose stark contrast between a loose lyrically flowing verse and a tight fitting lyric in the chorus, reinforced by a comparatively simpler melody and harmonic structure in the chorus, as compared to the verse.

A loose lyrical fit has the ability to suggest the natural phrasing of spoken dialogue. There's a comfortable, familiar feel to how the words flow freely across the beat. Because it's delivered as an almost spoken phrase, it holds the potential of intimacy and authenticity – like the words of a friend relaying a personal story in close quarters. These are powerful attributes that can be put to good use when you're trying to impart thoughts and emotions in a song.

On the other hand, there's a different kind of emphatic confidence and authority that can be implied by the rigid, declarative style of a tight lyrical fit, especially if they're sung by a British anarcho-punk band from the 90's. Think of the declarative chorus to Chumbawamba's 'Tubthumping' which locks into a rigid, rapid-fire beat with almost military precision:

I get knocked down
But I get up again
You're never gonna keep me down

The attributes and qualities I'm describing here don't always hold true, but there is a distinct qualitative difference between the two lyrical approaches and if nothing else they're worth experimenting with. You may be surprised at the results.

> *"Writing a song is like playing a series of downs in football: Lots of rules, timing is crucial, lots of boundaries, lots of protective gear, lots of stopping and starting. The upside is that there's no risk of concussion."*
> - Christine Lavin

- **PAINTING PICTURES** (Imagery) – *Are you painting a picture with your lyrics?* To my mind, the best songs transport the listener, and the best lyrics achieve this by using vivid imagery to set the scene. Details can help make a scene come alive.

This is admittedly a personal preference, but my favorite songwriters have always painted pictures with their lyrics, infusing their songs with vivid imagery, achieving an almost cinematic quality in their storytelling. It's something I've always aspired to do in my own writing - to paint pictures with lyrics. I try to achieve this in two ways: (1) by deploying all my senses to conjure up the scene in mind and (2) by incorporating as much *specificity* and *detail* as I can in order to paint those pictures.

It's a very deliberate process; picturing the scene, imagining not just the sights but the sounds, the smells, the tastes, the textures, the movement... I'm especially attuned to the lighting in a scene, which for me, helps to bring that scene to life. Just for the hell of it, I searched through my own catalog to locate instances in my lyrics where I referred to light in one form or another. This is just a partial list, but demonstrates how lighting – in one form or another – can play a key role in setting a scene. Each of the following lines is from a different song.

The only light a neon sign, flashing off and on...
When suddenly the light turned red...
My idea of having fun is laying naked in the sun with you...
The lights went on and they got up to go...
The golden arches light up the way...
I love the light in your eyes...
I sense the room awash in light...
And when the sun comes up I'm gonna take her home
the last faint ray of autumn light...
She goes to bed with the night light on...
And it seemed as if somehow the sun had bled...
We squabble and fight, we turn out the light...
A hunters moon sheds silver light...
She was a dauntless damsel with her lovelight all aglow...
I'm gonna turn off all the lights and crawl in bed...

The above lines may not make much sense taken out of context, but they do serve to illustrate the variety of ways in which different kinds of lighting can be employed to illuminate a scene.

Here's another example of lyric lighting by Joni Mitchell (also from 'A Case of You') doing it with more style (note: you'll recall from the preceding verse that if we want her she'll be in the bar. Well there she sits.):

On the back of a cartoon coaster
In the blue TV screen light
I drew a map of Canada
Oh, Canada
With your face sketched on it twice.

The scene she's painting is subtle, yet indelible. She's not evoking just any old light or lamp or bulb or glow, she's specifying an eerie kind of oversaturated but dim colored light that we're all vaguely familiar with having at least once in our lives found ourselves sitting in a curiously lit place exactly like that bar. With just a few lines, we've been transported.

> *"My style of songwriting is influenced by cinema. I'm a frustrated filmmaker. A fan once said to me, 'Girl, you make me see pictures in my head!' and I took that as a great compliment. That's exactly my intention."*
>
> - Joni Mitchell

It's this degree of specificity and detail that can help a listener see as well as hear the story being told. (If you try, you can even smell the stale beer in the verse.)

Of course, this doesn't mean every song has to be riddled with detail and populated with countless objects. A sparse lyric can have great resonance. And sometimes a sincere sentiment, simply expressed, is all that's required to do the job at hand.

This idea of using detail and specificity to *set the scene* is further expanded on in non-lyric forms of writing. It's expressed with a familiar writing adage, *show, don't tell*. The idea being that rather than bore your listener (or reader) with dry explanation (telling), it's better to provide them with interesting and relevant details that can help the listener/reader imagine what's going on (showing). Here's a simple example of telling: *He waited impatiently.* If you wanted to convey the same idea by showing, you might say: *His fingers drummed on the table incessantly, as he kept checking his watch, over and over again, his face contorting in ever increasing looks of concern.* 'Telling' expresses an idea by stating it in plain, simple terms. 'Showing' expresses the same idea in more detail and, hopefully, in more depth and with more color and insight. Note, however, that showing tends to use more words to make its point.

And that's where the familiar 'show don't tell' adage can become potentially problematic, as it relates to lyrics. Lyrics are more akin to poetry than other kinds of writing. And like poetry, lyrics usually benefit from brevity and the ability to distill ideas and descriptions into concise, tightly packed phrases. Showing can tend to take up a bit of space, so it's not always ideal in a lyric setting. This means you might need to allow more space when employing 'showing' in your lyrics. Alternatively, you'll need to 'show' in a tightly condensed, compact way.

Ed Sheeran accomplishes just that, with poignancy and grace in his stunning song, 'The A Team':

White lips, pale face
Breathing in snowflakes
Burnt lungs, sour taste
Light's gone, day's end
Struggling to pay rent
Long nights, strange men

With just a few carefully chosen words and sparse, condensed images, he manages to conjure up a stark and vivid world, and to evoke, with the briefest of descriptions, a fragile and tragic character. And he accomplishes this mostly by showing, with snap-shots and; and with hardly any telling.

> *"We are the Swiss watchmakers of music and literature."*
> – Jimmy Webb

In reality, the choice between showing and telling is a non-issue, because most writing incorporates both showing and telling (often at the same time). But it's definitely a good idea to at least have an understanding of the concept of *showing* – that is, being descriptive, or as I see it, painting pictures vs *telling* – giving just the facts, ma'am, just the facts.

In my own writing, I'm very aware of a strong tendency towards populating my lyrics with lots of seemingly ordinary details. For me, those concrete details help to fix the scene in the listeners' mind, while still allowing them to flesh out the story with their own imaginations. That's important. You want to the listener to be an active participant in a song. You want to draw them in as collaborators in a way. Provide them with the crucial details and let them fill in the blanks. In doing so, they'll be that much more engaged in the song. By inviting your audience to color in the missing parts of the picture you're painting, you allow them to become a part of the song.

The first line of my song, 'Lydia' begins,

> *Lydia keeps my toothbrush in her apartment and she never complains, well hardly ever...*

A toothbrush might seem a trivial object to feature in an opening line, but for me it serves to set the stage for the song by conjuring up not only a vivid image of the apartment but also suggesting the casual intimacy of the relationship.

I tend to think of my songs as short stories set to music. This is not always the case, but it's admittedly a big part of my personal songwriting style. And because I view them as *short* stories, it's a priority for me to sum things up quickly, and succinctly, whenever possible. Populating a lyric with specific, familiar and *relevant* objects helps me achieve that in a few words. And if those details and ordinary objects have strong associations attached to them, even better – it helps me cover even *more* ground in less space.

Here are the lyrics to my song, 'No School Today', which is kind of a tone poem (but with words) designed to conjure up the surprise and awe of waking up to a world completely transformed by a blanket of snow.

No School Today

Nestled snuggly in your arms
drifting lazily in and out of sleep
I reach across to quiet the alarm
a minute more our cozy den to keep

Then peering through half-opened eyes.
I sense the room awash in light.
And through the window see the sun
Reflected in a world of white.

I shake my head, roll out of bed
step onto the cold wood floor.
And to the window I am led
To find the world I knew was there no more

Instead, as far as the eye could see,
the land, the hills, the pond, the trees
was covered in a blanket white
With glistening silver finery.

The lady on the radio.
She said 'Jack Frost has come to play
She said, 'the roads are closed on account of snow'
She said, 'and yes, there is no school today.'

A wintry tableau of tranquility
Snow drifts covering the patio.
A tiny chipmunk darts into a tree
and leaves his footprints in the snow

I hear a snowplow up the street
The neighbor's dog begins to fret.
The alarm goes off at 6:15
And I climbed straight back into bed.

The telling version of this song would consist of the line 'gee, it snowed a lot last night', sung over and over again. Instead, I try to evoke all the jumbled feelings of confusion and wonder at discovering such a dramatic transformation in a still half-awake state. To do that, I describe a specific place – *our cozy den* - specific sights – *the land, the hills, the pond, the trees, glistening silver finery, the snow covered patio, a chipmunk's footprints* – the lighting– *awash in light, the sun reflected in a world of light* - and specific sounds – *a snowplow, a dog barking, the radio, the alarm* – all of which combine to conjure up a vision of not just the scene itself, but more importantly, of the experience of that scene.

Here's another example. In my song, 'Shopping Bag Ladies', I'm painting a familiar picture of a population of homeless women in a bus station. I rely on detail to describe my characters as well as their situation:

The shopping bag ladies, it's not that well known but they're
really in vogue.
The latest in fashions, their tastes are so true,
Sweat socks and sneakers, a sweater or two
And safely behind the walls they have made,

Secure in their brown paper barricades...

Their attire is simply stated, even mundane, and recognizable to everyone, but there's a reason I don't describe only one sweater. In suggesting 'a sweater *or two*', I try to evoke their very unique, makeshift, improvisational style of dress. And their shopping bags, which surround them, containing all their worldly possessions, function as more than just light-weight, cheap luggage – it's baggage in every sense of the word.

Every object contains its own potential story. Ordinary, everyday details are jam-packed with information and associations. Carefully inserting those objects and specific details into your lyrics can help you cover a lot of ground; can enable you to tell stories *within* your story. What's more, those familiar objects become access points for your listeners, enabling them to conjure up their own personal version of your song in their own imaginations.

> *"I think the more the listener can contribute to the song, the better; the more they become part of the song, and they fill in the blanks. Rather than tell them everything, you save your details for things that exist. Like what color the ashtray is. How far away the doorway was. So when you're talking about intangible things like emotions, the listener can fill in the blanks and you just draw the foundation."* — John Prine

SURPRISES and PUNCHLINES

When I sit down to write a song, there's one main question that I keep asking myself over and over again: what can I do here, at this point, to surprise the listener?

I don't want to terrify them, mind you, or disturb the overall flow of the song. But I'm always striving to do something unanticipated – pleasing, yes, but unexpected. It could be as simple as moving from a major chord to its minor, or an unusual, but still musical, melodic leap, or a subtle string of internal rhymes or an odd but useful metaphor, or a joke or a pun, or a dramatic punchline! I want to keep the song interesting.

It doesn't happen everywhere, but I'm always on the lookout for an appropriate place to surprise the listener; in other words, to do something different, original, new – something that will tickle the listener's ear and make them smile, or sigh, or nod in recognition, or, occasionally, feel a slight tug on their heartstrings. Sometimes I pull it off. Not always. Part of any songwriter's job is to keep trying.

In the pre-chorus to Lily Allen's terrific song, 'The Fear', she sneaks in a sly and pointed double pun with references to two national celebrity obsessed UK newspapers, the Sun and the Mirror:

> And I'll take my clothes off and it will be shameless
> 'Cause everyone knows that's how you get famous.
> I'll look at the sun and I'll look in the mirror...

Lily's not just being funny and clever here. The deceptively simple pun resonates with the chilling anxiety of a funhouse horror scene in which the infinitely reflected mirror images become threatening distortions of reality; the true cost of fame - fear.

There are small surprises and big surprises, and it's not always easy to come up with them on demand, but if you learn to hear them in other people's songs, you may find yourself starting to incorporate them in your own.

Take a few minutes and listen to the transcendent 'Unchained Melody' [by Alex North and Hy Zaret]. The Righteous Brothers or Roy Orbison's versions will do nicely (just try, if you can, to erase the 'Ghost' movie image of a shirtless Patrick Swayze playing handsies in pottery-wheel clay with a captivating Demi Moore). When the melody, towards the end of the song, hits a high 'e' on the line, 'I *need* your love', real magic happens (as opposed to the ghostly floating-penny trick in the film). We've been taken by surprise with an unexpected climax, that also happens to underline the main theme of the song.

COMEDY

Jokes and puns are a special case, in that they operate by the same rules in a song as they do in any standup routine. They require setup, timing and just the right delivery. If you ask a comic how they write a joke, they're likely to tell you, 'work backwards'. Start with the punchline and then figure out an artful way of getting there, that is, prepare the setup. The same rules apply to jokes, gags and puns in a song. It's pretty much the same as rhyming couplets where you're trying to find an initial rhyme to match an existing last rhyme in a couplet. You're working backwards in order to arrive at the end point.

The awesome, Randy Newman, sets us up for a great punchline chorus in his song, 'Political Science', about what he feels is America's misunderstood place in the world, when he sings…

No one likes us-I don't know why
We may not be perfect, but heaven knows we try
But all around, even our old friends put us down
Let's drop the big one and see what happens.

He then goes on to offer up his xenophobic fantasy of the consequences, and some of the positive benefits, of unleashing our nuclear arsenal on the rest of the planet:

Boom goes London and boom Paree
More room for you and more room for me

With his droll Louisiana drawl and amiable demeanor, he manages to make this modest proposal of mass destruction seem not quite as sinister as a straight read of the lyrics might suggest.

As with all comedy, context matters. Once he reveals his premise – you know, bombing the hell out of the rest of the world - every subsequent joke explodes out of the same hyperbolic formula.

There's an early Dylan song, 'Don't Think Twice, It's All Right', a definite fan favorite, and one I've always taken a strong liking to. It's basically a song in which he's ditching his latest partner, but instead of telling her face to face, he leaves her this song and then skedaddles down the road before she wakes up.

The last few lines read…

I ain't sayin' you treated me unkind

You could have done better but I don't mind
You just kinda wasted my precious time
But don't think twice, it's all right

One day while listening to the song, and enjoying it, as usual, I suddenly thought to myself, 'Wait a minute. Here he is going on about how everything's cool and no hard feelings, *'it's all right'*, sounding like a nice, empathetic guy and then he goes and ends the song with a surprising zinger, *'you just kinda wasted my precious time'*, which is, I guess, the '60's folk-singer's polite way of saying, *'fuck you, bitch, I'm outa here!'*.

At that moment, it dawned on me that the songwriter was just making a pretense of being a thoughtful and considerate, nice guy; you know, Mr. Innocent, just moseying down the road. *Actually*, I thought, he's being kind of an asshole in the song. In fact, you could say he was being a cowardly asshole by going out of his way to disguise that very fact and by trying to make himself look like the wronged party in this failed relationship. Not to mention the fact that he split without even saying goodbye.

So, I though, hmmm… what if Dylan had been just a little more honest about his true feelings, a bit more up front with the sentiments he's expressing to his soon-to-be ex. So I sat down and wrote a song, a kind of pointed homage to 'Don't Think Twice, It's All Right)', titled, 'I Never Really Liked You All That Much'.

I offer up this example for a few reasons. One, you can be inspired by anything, at any time, and for any ridiculous reason. Two, 'I Never Really Liked You All That Much', derives all its laughs from a single premise, as does the Randy Newman's 'Political Science' example I just described. And, three, in live performance, 'I Never Really Liked You All That Much' gets more laughs per minute than any other song in my repertoire and is always a useful addition to a live set, so I figure it might have some value as I describe my recollection of the process of writing it.

As I've said from the beginning, the sooner you know what your song is about, the better. And I knew exactly what the song was about. Its theme was derived from what I took to be the true sentiment behind, 'Don't Think Twice, It's All Right', which in exaggerated form, and using the same kind of throw-away-line vernacular, became 'I Never Really Liked You All That Much'.

So, I started filling up pages with rhyming couplets that played on that sentiment; of someone I got involved with but that, in fact, I really couldn't stand. And I made a special effort to come up with a bunch of put-downs that were so over-the-top ridiculous that it would be hard to take them too seriously:

I Never Really Liked You All That Much

I see your favorite picture is no longer on the wall.
I couldn't help but notice all your luggage in the hall.
Before you head off on your way.
There's one thing I'd like to say...

    I'm not sorry to see you go.
    Don't bother to stay in touch.
    There's one thing you oughta know, sweet darlin'.
    I never really liked you all that much.

I got no regrets. Well, maybe just a few.
Like the day you were born and the day that I met you.
I should have nipped it in the bud.
The first time I noticed you were chewin' your cud.

And if the truth be known. You were not my first choice.
When you answered the phone. I thought it was your roommate's voice.
I meant to date her instead. But I wound up in bed with the wrong coed.

    I'm not sorry to see you go...

Don't think this failed relationship is a reflection of your worth.
It's just you come from where you do and I come from... Earth.
And maybe the only reason for this little glitch.
Is the fact that you're a stupid bitch.

I'm not being cruel. That never was my goal.
I realize that at heart you're just a sensitive soul.

I notice your psoriasis has worsened.
You know, it really couldn't happen to a nicer person.

And darling, if I may, forgive my being blunt.
But, I've just got to say...
You are a miserable...(uh)... person.
I don't mean to make disparaging remarks.
But in this light you resemble Groucho Marx

And please don't be insulted if I never want to see ya.
It's got nothing whatever to do with that time you gave
me gonorrhea.
I just need to make a brand new start.
With a woman who actually has a heart.

> *I'm not sorry to see you go.*
> *Don't bother to stay in touch.*
> *There's one thing you oughta know, sweet darlin'.*
> *I never really liked you all that much.*

Now, I have to stress that in crafting the lyrics to this song, I also tried very hard to adhere to what I took to be the underlying sentiment and tone of the original, which is essentially that of an unreliable narrator, relentlessly dissing this poor woman while making pretenses to being a nice guy. So, just like with Dylan's caveat, *'I'm not saying you treated me unkind...'*, my version prefaces every put-down with some completely disingenuous denial such as,

> *I'm not being cruel. That never was my goal.*
> *I realize that at heart you're just a sensitive soul...*

Or I'd set up a diss with a seemingly magnanimous preface like,

> *Don't think this failed relationship is a reflection of your*
> *worth.*
> *It's just you come from where you do... and I come from*
> *Earth.*

Admittedly, the poison barbs in my song are a bit more blatant than Dylan's, but that was by design. Yet, I still maintain that both songs are expressing a strikingly similar sentiment, one perhaps more artfully than the other. ;-) And I'll make another important point, which is that I stuck to my guns: meaning that once I came up with a premise (well, actually co-opted one), I made a determined effort to stay true to that premise; every line of the song relates to the original theme, which gives the song a cohesiveness and internal logic. It's also where all the jokes come from.

Now some might argue that it was impertinent, presumptuous, foolhardy and arrogant of me to attempt what's basically a comic re-write of an iconic Dylan song – and they would be right. But I have to say, I had a helluva fun time doing so, and I highly recommend you all consider doing the same, just for the heady experience. Besides, whenever I'm on tour, it never fails to crack up the audience, night after night.

Before I move on to the next section, I'm going to squeeze one more educational tidbit out of, 'I Never Really Liked You All That Much', which deals with the idea of overwriting, editing and self-censorship.

I've talked before about overwriting and how it can be a useful practice to generate more ideas than you can actually use. Although, it then requires that you practice lyrical triage in order to get rid of the stuff that you don't absolutely need. That was the case in 'I Never Really Liked You...' In the process of whittling down the lyrics, I managed to get rid of two or three verses, in part, by combining them into one. The remaining verse, which does not appear above or in the recorded version of the song was as follows:

'I'm not saying we didn't have a lot of fun.
Like the time you got your tit stuck in my accordion.
You should have seen the look on your face.
They could hear you scream in outer space.

The problem came when I played the song for my wife and teenage daughter, who laughed throughout the song, until I came to that verse, at which point their scowls of disapproval prompted me to take one defensive step backwards, for fear of what might happen next. I was told in no uncertain terms that I couldn't possibly keep the offensive verse in the song. Now, I'm not, normally, that easily dissuaded, especially when it comes to my music, and besides, I was especially proud of my deft use of hyperbole, demonstrated by the idea that you could hear the *scream in outer space*. Because, as you well know, they *can't* actually hear you scream in the vacuum of outer space. (Unless, of course, you're screaming into a radio headset in your space helmet, or maybe using sign language, which doesn't really count, and would probably just send you flailing off into to the void, anyway).

So, un-swayed, I proceeded to perform the song for a few local audiences to see how folks liked the song, in general, and especially to test out their reaction to the now problematic 'accordion' verse.

The song got loads of laughs, but every time I sang that particular verse, a curious thing happened: the guys in the audience would crack up in a burst of explosive laughter, while the women in the audience would groan in disbelief, and shake their heads at me in disgust and dismay.

There was a definite gender split in how folks reacted to the song. Half my audience found the line hilarious, while the other half wanted to strangle me with my guitar strap.

I dropped the verse.

I only relate this anecdote to touch briefly on the issue of self-censorship. Every songwriter has to make that judgment call for themselves as to what is warranted and where they draw the line between free artistic expression and what's deemed appropriate in a public setting. [ie. how much of their audience they're willing to alienate.]

When Randy Newman had his first big commercial hit with his song, 'Short People', he undoubtedly offended a whole lot of folks of diminutive stature. And even though the song's satirical bent was unmistakable, there's also no question that many little people considered the song to be a clear instance of sizeism and discrimination. I love the song, but I acknowledge that it has the potential to cause offense and genuine emotional pain to the population who are its target, and certainly the question of how a young little person might feel upon hearing the song, out of any adult comedic context, deserves consideration.

Having said that, I will always defend Randy Newman's absolute right to expressing himself the way he does. First of all, he's great at it, expounding on a variety of social and interpersonal issues with artfulness and his unique brand of sly, wry humor. Second of all, he's willing to say things, in his inimitable way, that still need to be said, and that most people still shy away from. He says them with courage, with deft humor and with heart. Do you really believe he's actually proposing we drop nuclear weapons on all the countries that annoy us? Anyone familiar with his work and his seriocomic satirical style knows that his songs speak out against all types of insanity, injustice and prejudice, and that what his song, 'Short People', actually stands for is the complete opposite of prejudice, instead highlighting and making fun of the sheer absurdity of our wrongheaded preconceptions and stereotypes. But to get all that, you have to listen.

Just something to think about. Ultimately, as a writer, as an artist, what you choose say is up to you. Just be prepared for the consequences.

"All is fair in love and songwriting." - Norah Jones

PUNNISHING PUNS

Nothing is guaranteed to make an audience either groan or laugh louder than a well-placed pun. Basically a pun squeezes humor out of a word that has two different meanings (called a homonym). A pun can also be created from two words that sound alike (called a homophone) but are spelled differently and, also have two different meanings.

Puns don't necessarily have to be funny. Poems, and virtually every line of Shakespeare are filled with words that have double meanings. Call them puns or homonyms or homophones... they tickle your brain, they illuminate a passage, they remind us that things are never quite as simple as they seem and that a seemingly innocuous phrase may actually have a deeper meaning.

We've already made mention of a number of puns, but just for the hell of it, here's a silly musician joke that's built around a slightly painful pun:

I started a band called 999 Megabytes — only problem is, we haven't got a gig yet.

So, yeah, as you already know full well, puns can evoke groans, giggles, belly laughs or smiles. Sometimes they can even offer a sly way to provide pertinent information about a character in a song.

Consider this half verse from my first single, 'Ariel', which concludes with a pun; a pun that also serves to reveal – to *'show'* – just what a free-spirit the song's leading lady, Ariel, was.

I took a shower and I put on my best blue jeans.
I picked her up in my new VW van.
She wore a peasant blouse with nothing underneath.
I said, "Hi". She said, "Yeah, I guess I am."

To my surprise and amusement, this light-hearted bit of sung dialogue became a catch-phrase at shopping malls and summer camps, across America, the summer the single hit the charts. But let me pause here, for a moment, to make something perfectly clear.

I know that throughout the pages of this book, I keep stressing the idea that the craft of songwriting involves making conscious choices about how your song evolves. But you'll also recall me saying that sometimes songs write themselves.

What I'm trying to say is this: When I wrote those lyrics to Ariel, I was definitely *not* making a conscious decision to 'show-not-tell'. I was definitely *not* making a deliberate choice to populate the lyric with lots of colorful detail. And I was absolutely *not* making a calculated decision to invent some kind of herbal pun as a punchline to that stanza – it just happened, a happy accident which I immediately recognized as a 'keeper'. I wasn't thinking about idiom or rhyme scheme or key or tempo or persona or setting the scene. The fact is, I was improvising and goofing around and writing by intuition and the only credit I'm willing to give myself, in retrospect, in terms of craft, is having been able to recognize, at the time, which accidental lines just happened to work really well.

So, why am I advising you to make conscious choices while at the same time admitting that I didn't do any of that in one of my earlier songwriting efforts?

Because, as I continued to write more and more songs, I gradually began to notice the various kinds of musical and lyrical choices I was making unconsciously, intuitively and inadvertently, all along. I became aware of those choices *in retrospect*. And as soon as I realized the kinds of choices I was making, over and over again, it finally dawned on me that I could make those same choices on purpose – consciously, deliberately – instead of always being completely at the mercy of my muse. That's when I was able to gradually begin applying craft to my songwriting, to begin to exercise *slightly* more control over the creative process.

Again, that's all this book is about: my attempt to describe the various choices you can make in order to influence how your songs evolve and take shape.

But remember, *for goodness sakes*, don't ever abandon the unconscious, intuitive, inadvertent, *inspired* aspect of your songwriting; that's where all the juicy bits come from.

At the same time, keeping all of those choices in the back of your mind – all of that craft - can help facilitate the writing process, can help make you a better songwriter.

And, if you just happen to find yourself stuck with a troublesome phrase or a pesky rhyme, or a hard-to-resolve chord progression, if you find you've painted yourself into a corner in the middle of your song... understanding what some of your songwriting options are, and knowing what questions to ask yourself, might just provide the answer you need to paint yourself right out of that corner.

THE FEINT (misdirection)

Another common comedy device which pops up in songs is the feint, in which you lead your listing quarry to believe you're about to sing one thing, but then go ahead and do another. It's misdirection – a songwriter's magic trick - and often relies on the assumption that the person listening has a dirty mind (or at least knows how to rhyme). The trick is you're getting your listener to sing a word in their head that you never actually sing.

Here's a couplet by the awesome, Meghan Trainor, from her song, 'Dear Future Husband':

> *I'll be sleeping on the left side of the bed*
> *Open doors for me and you might get some... kisses*

Oddly, all the other couplets that came before that one, rhymed!

I execute a similar feint, with much less panache, in 'I Never Really Liked You All That Much' with the couplet:

> *And darling, if I may, forgive my being blunt.*
> *But, I've just got to say...*
> *You are a miserable...(uh)... person.*

What can I say? Be sure and carry your poetic license wherever you go!

SURPRISE ENDINGS – I'll have mine with a twist!

I've mentioned earlier that I often think of my songs as short stories set to music.

And like some short stories with a surprise ending, there is a whole category of story songs that do pretty much the same thing - hold off revealing their surprise 'til the very end.

One of the best known songs with a twist is the Kink's fun loving, 'Lola' [Ray Davies] in which a naïve young man meets a sultry lass in a club only to discover by the end of the night the real reason Lola '...*walked like a woman and talked like a man.*' Which the young man finally reveals in the last verse:

> *Well I'm not the world's most masculine man*
> *But I know what I am and I'm glad I'm a man*
> *And so is Lola*
> *La-la-la-la Lola   la-la-la-la Lola*

And of course, there's Rupert Holmes', 'Escape (The Piña Colada Song)' in which a dissatisfied guy responds to a personal ad in the paper (unbeknownst to his current partner), which reads,

If you like piña coladas and taking walks in the rain
If you're not into yoga. If you have half a brain.
If you like making love at midnight, on the dunes of the
cape.
I'm the love that you've looked for. Write to me and
escape!

The unwitting Romeo arranges to meet up with the ad's writer, only to discover – in the last verse - that it's his equally frustrated partner who placed the ad. They supposedly have a laugh over it and down some drinks then, presumably, head out to the nearest sand dune for some midnight nookie.

Head south, below the Mason-Dixon line and you'll find songs like 'The Night the Lights Went Out in George' [by Bobby Russell], a Southern Gothic tale about adultery and murder, that only reveals the real killer until the last verse (spoiler alert: the narrator did it).

Or another classic, 'Ode to Billy Joe' [by Bobbie Gentry] which leaves the actual reason for Billy Joe's suicide somewhat vague, but does reveal in the very last verse that (once again) the song's narrator may have played a key role in why *'...Billy Joe MacAllister jumped off the Tallahatchie Bridge'*.

Eminem's disturbingly twisted 'Stan' [by Eminem aka Marshall Mathers], is another 'song with a twist' that comes to mind, where in the final verse it finally dawns on the song's narrator that the unsettling fan-mail he's been answering was written by some guy, who the news recently reported, drove himself and his pregnant wife off a bridge. I guess you'd have to call this an example of Mid-Western Gothic.

And one of my favorites is the delightful, 'Chuck E's in Love' [by Rickie Lee Jones], which spends several verses wondering why Chuck E's been acting so strange and then ends with the giddy revelation that…

Chuck E's in love with the little girl who's singing this
song

Like most songs with a surprise or plot twist ending – comedy or drama - these songs were written backwards.

Everything leading up to the final reveal is a set-up, strategically designed to prepare the listener for that reveal. Sometimes, not always, the writer will provide a few subtle clues about what's really going on, but not enough to give anything away until the very end.

In my song, 'The Dolphins Were Dancing', I paint a vivid picture of a multitude of creatures of every description, on land and at sea, letting loose in an ecstatic, celebratory frenzy...

> *And the sky was filled with birds for a thousand miles.*
> *And the platypuses played along the shore with the crocodiles.*
> *And a hundred thousand whales were balancing on their tails*
> *and the starfish and the clams were in a circle holding hands with the oysters and the snails*
>
> *And the dolphins were dancing...*

The upbeat musical groove serves to further support the festive, euphoric mood of all these party animals, until it's finally revealed to the listener, just why all these creatures are celebrating:

> *And as the evening fell, the sky turned red And it seemed as if somehow the sun had bled.*
> *And I stared into the eyes of a million fire flies. And I heard an eagle say, "We celebrate this day man has finally passed away."*
>
> *And the dolphins were dancing...*

Permit me a quick aside in regards to this song, which has nothing to do with the immediate topic at hand, but pertains to how long some songs take to write.

I started writing 'The Dolphins Were Dancing' while studying music at the City College of New York, sometime around 1975. I was taking the subway home after classes, but accidently slept through my stop, finally waking up alone in the subway car, which was now sitting stationary, parked in a dark, underground transfer depot.

As I sat contemplating my predicament, a conductor walked through, saw me, and explained that the train would be back in service in another 20 minutes and to just sit tight and wait. Which I did. Underground. In a dark train depot. For 20 minutes. In retrospect, I did what anyone would do in those circumstances; I fantasized about being absolutely anywhere else other than where I was at that moment. I pictured an idyllic island setting, with sparkling white sanded beaches, swaying palm trees, and a pod of dolphins dancing in the surf.

Somehow, that image stuck with me and after 20 minutes of nervous waiting, the subway car finally headed back into service with a lurching jolt. When I finally exited the subway and reached the sunlit surface, I tore a piece of scrap paper out of my knapsack and wrote the words, 'The Dolphins Were Dancing'. When I arrived home that night I glanced at the piece of paper and shoved it in a top desk drawer where I kept all my assorted scraps of paper, menus, napkins, matchbook covers and placemats, all covered with song sketches and stray rhymes or scribbled musical phrases.

Every now and then, I'd open that drawer and sift through some of the sketches to see if anything happened to grab my imagination enough to compel me to finish it, and every now and then, something would. Twenty years later I found that scrap of paper and decided it was time I finally turned that evocative line into a song.

Once I made that commitment, my first order of business was clear: I had to ask the obvious question: Why were the dolphins dancing?

Once I arrived at the answer to that question my path was clear. I knew what the song was about, and with that goal in mind, I had a simple strategy for finishing it. I worked backwards towards the predetermined punchline (our eventual demise) and structured verse after verse that would deceive the listener into a pastoral vision of a peaceable kingdom, only to reach its doomsday conclusion. Doomsday for us, that is. The animals live on to party hardy, dancing the Macarena, or possible the Twist – the surprise ending, *plot* twist.

Here are my reasons for relaying this story. (1) Write everything down and shove it in a drawer (or a folder on your desktop). Go back and look at your sketches every now and then, because the odds are that, eventually, you'll find something you actually like enough to complete, and when you do... (2) Ask yourself questions about your source material. The answers to those questions will tell you what your song is about and... (3) Once you know what your song is about, you'll have a goal and a strategy for finishing the song, which is basically to write a page filled with lines and couplets that relate to the main premise and then whittle them down into a song.

We'll continue to revisit that basic formula from various perspectives, but for now let's talk about some aspects of a song that are a little difficult to define.

AUTHENTICITY, SINCERITY & HEART

Your song might be masterfully crafted and chock-full-of clever rhymes and chord changes, but if something about it seems counterfeit, if its intention feels insincere, and if it fails to move the listener, you've left out three of a song's most important ingredients.

Sure, there are plenty of successful songs that get by without these key attributes; some may even be pretty good songs. But to my mind, a great song has all three.

These attributes are important because they make it possible for your audience to connect. The notes and words may be important but the emotions they evoke are more important. How a song makes you feel is what matters most.

That's just my humble opinion and in truth these kinds of nebulous, hard-to-define emotional attributes can be extremely subjective.

If I had to boil it down to one overriding piece of advice, I'd say be *honest* in your songwriting. That doesn't mean you can't lie and make things up – that's what your poetic license is for (which, by the way, I always keep in my back pocket, within easy reach, in case I'm stopped by the grammar police for reckless alliteration or punning a red light). And it doesn't mean you can't embellish and exaggerate like an over-enthusiastic second grader trying to impress his schoolmates on the first day of class (that's hyperbole).

But it's my experience that a song will always stand a better chance of connecting with your audience if you speak from your heart. Say what you mean. It doesn't necessarily have to be overt, but tell the truth as you believe it.

People respond strongly to things they recognize as real, as authentic, especially if it relates to their own experience. If a song seems real as well as familiar, it will resonate. It will strike a chord in the listener.

Also, speaking from your heart grants you a kind of authority, an authority based on sincerity and conviction. A song that possess those attributes, has a confidence and a certainty that can compel listeners to temporarily surrender their preconceptions and prejudices, and take on board what's being said with fresh, unbiased ears.

I'm going to refrain from offering a slew of examples, here, of songs that I feel possess elements of authenticity, sincerity and heart.

Instead, think of the songs that meant the most to you when you first heard them, that still mean the most to you. And then consider what were the key ingredients that made those songs resonate within you.

I will point to a certain category of Artists, singers who are also songwriters: folks like Annie Lennox, John Prine, Nina Simone, Johnny Cash, Adele, Willie Nelson, Pink, Bruce Springsteen, Billy Holiday, Leonard Cohen, Lou Reed, Chrissie Hynde, and David Bromberg, just to name a few. There are plenty more like them, and I'm sure you can make a list of your own. Believability is what they all have in common. When they sing a song, you don't doubt that they mean it. You naturally assume that they believe every word they're singing, and because of that, you believe it too. This quality – sincerity, honesty - is characteristic of a good singer and performer, but it's also a characteristic of a good song.

You might think I'm referring only to heavy, serious, somber songs, but I'm not. What I'm saying here is true even of seemingly frivolous comedy songs. It's just that you might have to dig a little deeper to find those key ingredients.

One of my favorite comedy songs of all time is a song by Dana Lyons called, 'Cows With Guns'. It's absurd and hilarious and filled with awful puns and it's pure genius (brilliant video too). Be sure to check it out. But as silly as its premise is, there's a sustained truthfulness to the storyline and telling of the tale. The internal logic of this inane fantasy never falters. You could do a detailed analysis of its deeper meaning, the extended metaphors, the possible indictment of industrial farming and/or America's gun culture, but you'd be missing the point. The song feels perversely true. It's power is in the fact that you can actually imagine the crazy scenario of a herd of cows picking up firearms and heroically fighting for their inalienable right to be free, or more to the point, to avoid winding up between two halves of a hamburger bun.

Seriously.

CLICHÉ's – AVOID 'EM or NOT!?

One of the hardest parts of writing a good song is trying to come up with new, original stuff while avoiding old, hackneyed phrases, overly used idiomatic expressions and clichés.

Avoiding clichés is itself a cliché. And for the most part it's good advice. You *should* strive for originality in both your lyrics and your musical ideas. You don't want to put your listeners to sleep by dishing up a bunch of stale ideas they've heard over and over again, a thousand times before. You don't want to bore your audience to death with a cliché. Definitely not. Avoid 'em.

Unless you're Bob Dylan, of course.

Now, let me be clear: I don't want to give Bob a hard time. He's one of my favorite songwriters. He's a legend for goodness sakes!

But here's an irrefutable truth: a surprising number of Dylan's most popular, and highly regarded songs were built upon idiomatic expressions and turns of phrase that have been in common use in the English language for hundreds of years. Here's just a partial list of the titles of well-known Bob Dylan songs which were crafted out of commonly used idiomatic expressions, which could legitimately be considered clichés:

'Don't Think Twice (It's All Right)'
'Don't Think Twice': an idiomatic expression in common use since the early 1900's.

'Shelter From the Storm'
'Shelter From the Storm': an idiomatic expression in common use since the early 1800's

'Forever Young'
'Forever Young': an idiomatic expression in common use since the late 1800's.

'Knock, Knock, Knockin' on Heaven's Door'
'Kocking at Heaven's Door': an idiomatic and religious expression in common use since the early 1800's.

'I Shall Be Released'
'I Shall Be Released': (also 'Ye Shall Be Release') an idiomatic and religious expression in common use since the 1700's.

'On a Night Like This'
'On a Night Like This': an idiomatic expression in common use since the 1700's.

'Like a Rolling Stone'
'Like a Rolling Stone': an idiomatic and religious expression in common use since the 1600's; and a common blues and country idiom used in songs by Muddy Waters and Hank Williams, among many others.

Notice a pattern here? Some of Dylan's most famous songs were built on oft used clichés.

Again, just to be clear, this is not a criticism – it's a compliment.

Here's why:

The point is not to avoid using clichés. Sure, avoid 'em as much as you can, but the more important lesson here is this: if you're going to use a cliché, use it well. Make it your own. Write a song that justifies that cliché. Write a song that is so good that the listener doesn't even notice the cliché, forgets all about it, imagines that they'd never heard the expression before, are only hearing it now for the very first time.

This is a crucial point. And one which applies to music as well as lyric.

> NOTE: Crafting compelling songs out of cliché is no mean trick, and it's not just a habit of Dylan's, by the way; you see it frequently in country music, especially, where well-worn, familiar phrases - clichés - are given a new lease on life by clever repurposing in a brand new setting: Songs like, 'The Whiskey Ain't Working Anymore', 'Toeing the Line', 'A Guy Walks Into a Bar', 'Don't Let Me Be Lonely',' The Heart Won't Lie', 'Not a Moment Too Soon', 'She Keeps The Home Fires Burning', ' Behind Closed Doors' 'I Can't Stop Loving You', just scratch the surface of popular country songs, whose titles are derived from familiar expressions. It's O.K. to use something familiar, that people can immediately relate to, so long as you provide an original context for it, give it a brand new setting.

I'm sure Bob will forgive me using his music as an example, to make one more related point (you can take it, Bob!). Consider this:

It's pretty common knowledge, at least in the folk community, that Dylan's, 'Blowin' in the Wind', one of his most iconic songs, and an anthem of the 1960's civil rights movement, was lifted almost note for note from an old Negro spiritual, "No More Auction Block", that traces its origins back to the 1800's. Dylan has always acknowledge this and you can hear recordings of him performing the song at the Gaslight in Greenwich Village. In truth, none of this should be shocking; adapting and fashioning new songs from old songs is a long held and respected folk music tradition.

Which brings us right back to a point I made at the beginning of this book: Steal with humility (and stealth). And try to choose your influences carefully.

Dylan's a magpie; he collects turns of phrase, choice expressions and musical ideas from a slew of influences – then he *makes them his own.* Transforms them into something original. That's more important that whether you make use of a cliché or shoplift a familiar chord progression. It doesn't matter where your ideas came from – what matters is what you do with them.

INIMITABLE STYLES

Throughout this book, I've pointed to numerous examples by many respected songwriters in an attempted to illustrate what I view as some of the standard tools of the songwriting trade. But, as I said at the outset, even though we can always draw valuable lessons from examining another writer's work, I could really only guess at how their songs came about, and even then I don't really presume to know how they do what they do, or what they had in mind when they were writing a particular song. Of course, I went and guessed anyway, to illustrate various points about the craft and, hopefully, to provide you with some insights into the songwriting process.

But there are certain songwriters, whose styles are so individual and so atypical – so wonderfully different – that I can't even begin to guess how they do it.

One such songwriter that comes to mind is the great Laura Nyro.

For me, at least, her songs, all of them, defy any analysis or attempt to understand how she might have composed them. So, I've given up even trying. Which is probably for the best. Their structure both obeys and disregards convention. They're simultaneously familiar and unfamiliar. And somehow these indefinable songs possess an hypnotic beauty that compels a listener to surrender completely to the world she creates. Here's a verse of her, 'Stoned Soul Picnic', which, at first glance, seems like a simple, innocuous lyric…

> *Can you surry? Can you picnic?*
> *Can you surry? Can you picnic?*
> *Come on, come on, let's surry down to a stoned soul picnic*
> *Surry down to a stoned soul picnic*

There'll be lots of time and wine

Red, yellow, honey, sassafras and moonshine
Red, yellow, honey, sassafras and moonshine
Stoned soul, stoned soul

Listen to any recording of Stoned Soul Picnic. It's one of her least complex songs, yet compelling in a way I can't begin to explain. I wish I could help. But, in this case, you're on your own. You'd do well to listen to her whole catalog. Songs like, 'Wedding Bell Blues', 'Eli's Comin'', 'Stony End', 'And When I Die' are precious, idiosyncratic masterpieces and, truthfully, it boggles the mind that the mainstream music business ever allowed them on the radio.

> *"There are no limitations with a song. To me a song is a little piece of art. It can be whatever you like it to be. You can write the simplest song, and that's lovely, or you can just write a song that is abstract art."* - Laura Nyro

Leonard Cohen is another songwriter I would put in this uncategorizable category. One of a kind. Impossible to define. A poet who won't acknowledge being one. A singer who claims to not be able to carry a tune. His songs belong to no discernable idiom, are often difficult to interpret and yet they hit you in the gut. It's said he wrote as many as 80 verses to his classic, 'Hallelujah', before paring it down and finally recording it. Talk about lyrical triage!

> *"Journalists, especially English journalists, were very cruel to me. They said I only knew three chords when I knew five!* - Leonard Cohen

If I started describing the songwriting virtues of Joni Mitchell, her uncompromising originality, and her influence on every songwriter of my generation, I wouldn't know where to stop. She's the High-Priestess of Singer-Songwriters.

And then there's the wonderful Anita Baker, who besides having a voice as mellifluous as honey, writes songs in her own hybrid R&B/jazz/pop idiom that combine a sublime lyrical purity with a rich harmonic and melodic complexity, virtually unheard of in popular music.

I could easily add to this list, but my main point in identifying these songwriters, in particular, was to reiterate and underline the idea that while I hope you find some value in all of the pointers, suggestions and advice presented in this book, at some point, it's up to *you* to make your own rules, develop your own style, and speak with your own unique and individual voice.

New generations of songwriters continue to break conventions, invent new forms, create hybrid styles and define their own genres. Songwriters like Regina Spektor, Ed Sheeran, Fiona Bevan, Jeremy Larson, Claire Healy, Jason Mraz, Lana Del Rey, Rufus Wainwright, Esperanza Spalding, Lach and Pat Monahan (Train) - to name just a few of the multitude of talented songwriters out there, producing work of striking originality - carry the spark of individualism and undeniable style that bodes well for the future of songwriting. There are many thousands more out there - still unknown, yet undiscovered, honing their craft, writing great songs - that are every bit as talented as the artists I just named. Some of them are reading these very words! ;-)

'LIVE' PERFORMANCE

Not everyone sings their own songs. But the singer-songwriter era spawned a generation of songwriters who wrote especially personal songs; songs that, because they'd written themselves, and had first-hand knowledge of, they sang with an intimacy and believability that helped those songs ring true.

Of course, being a songwriter doesn't make you a great interpreter of your own songs, and you don't have to be a songwriter to sing with profound emotion.

But it's worth thinking about the crucial connection between the words of a song and how they are sung.

Not every good song has to possess the qualities of authenticity, sincerity and heart, mentioned earlier, but those that do stand an easier chance of being relatable, of connecting and resonating with an audience.

To my mind, the job of a singer is to give respect to the song, whether they wrote it or not. A singer achieves this by believing in what they are singing. It's an actor's job which relies, not on counterfeit emotions, but on becoming the character in the song and sincerely and honestly speaking/singing in that character's voice. If a singer does their job well and believes in what they are singing, the listening audience will believe it too.

So, anyone that is writing and singing their own songs has a bit of head-start in this regards, regardless of whether they sing in dulcet tones or not. If you are honest in your writing, it can make it easier for you to recall those thoughts and feelings when you open your mouth to sing. But even then, it's not necessarily an easy thing to do.

My biggest challenge as a performer is to mean what I say when I sing the words I wrote. Any experienced performer can fake sentiment and emotion, and generally succeed in convincing most of the audience, but the best performers aren't faking it; they may be calculated about when they breath and how long they sustain a note and how much vibrato they introduce at a certain point, but if they're doing their job they're also singing with sincerity and honesty – they mean what they sing.

And in order for anyone to mean what they sing or say, they have to deliver their lines as if they were speaking them for the first time to a loved one or a friend.

With all the inherent distractions of being on stage, or in a studio – lights, audience noise, mics, cables, etc... - it's hard for even an experienced performer to sustain that level of sincerity for any length of time. But that's the job. And like I said, it's not always easy.

There's one song of mine, 'I'm a Lucky Guy', which I generally place in the middle of my show, which is a simple, country tune that expresses my genuine view, despite my many complaints and frustrations, of my relative good fortune. You could say it's corny, but audiences seem to enjoy and relate to it.

I'm a lucky guy.
Got a wife just as sweet as Apple Pie.
Well, sometimes she can be a little tart but I cannot lie...

I'm a lucky guy.

I'm a lucky guy.
Don't have much money and I don't know why.
'cause I work real hard and god knows I try. But, even so…
I'm a lucky guy.

I am a lucky guy, I'm a fortunate son of a gun.
You might have a billion bucks, but.
Your life's not half as fun.

I'm a lucky guy.
I wake up every morning I can see the sky.
The sun may not be shining now, but it will be by and by and I…
I'm a lucky guy…

Though, sometimes, it seems I'm just barely squeaking by.
Then I catch a glimpse of my sweetheart, out of the corner of my eye. And I know…
I'm a lucky guy.

I've had my share of troubles, I've had my share of woe.
But when all is said and done…
One thing for sure I know…

I'm a lucky guy.
I've got my friends and family nearby.
Some guys have a little luck, but mine's in vast supply, 'cause I…
I'm a lucky guy.

I'm a lucky guy.
It may not be that visible to the naked eye.
But I have been so blessed, I cannot deny, that I…
I'm a lucky guy.

Though there are days, it seems most everything's goin' wrong.
I guess I could complain,
Instead I sing this song.

I'm a lucky guy

There's nothing I really need that I can't buy.
I've got food and drink to fill me up and shelter to stay dry. Truth
be told...
I'm a lucky guy...

I don't take it for granted and I'll tell you why...
'Cause I know it could all be gone in the blink of an eye. And I...
I'm a lucky guy.

I place this song in the middle of my set, because whenever I'm standing on stage, singing that particular song, my guitar in hand, looking out over an audience - no matter how large or small - it's impossible for me to not reconnect with the powerful personal truth behind every word of the song. Which is essentially, that as long as I'm still here, surrounded by loving family and friends, healthy and able, against all odds, to make even a modest living pursuing my music, I am, indeed, a 'lucky guy'.

For some reason, that particular song, forces me to sing honestly and sincerely, even on those occasional nights, where everything seems to be going wrong and I find myself distracted and in a lousy mood. I can sometimes feel my voice actually reconnect with all those feelings of gratitude expressed in the song's lyric, so that for those fleeting moments, I'm genuinely meaning what I say, and singing what I mean.

And when I finally get to the punchline in the last verse, *"...cause I know it could all be gone in the blink of an eye.",* if I'm doing my job right, the whole audience believes what I'm saying too, because they know it to be just as true for them as it is for me. And at that moment, we're all on the same page, all in this together, all part of the same song.

So try to keep some of this stuff in mind when you're writing *and* singing. Words have meaning. At least in this part of the world, you can't get arrested for singing what you believe, so you might as well express yourself as truthfully and honestly as you can. Unless, of course, you're using poetic license, to lie and make things up, which is totally cool, as well. Really, there are no fast and fixed rules to any of this. Maybe one - try not to be boring.

I'll describe this as the Horton the Elephant method of

songwriting and singing with veracity, ala Dr. Suess, in which Horton so eloquently put it, where he, *'...meant what he said and he said what he meant.'* Sage advice from a pachyderm who's *'faithful one hundred percent!'*

WHEN YOUR SONG FLIES THE COOP

Something remarkable occurs once you've finished a song and released it out into the world. It doesn't matter whether you perform it on live TV in front of millions of people, or in the den for your kid sister and your dog.

The fact is, once your song has been heard by someone else, in a way, it's no longer your own. Anyone that hears it will interpret it in their own peculiar way, understanding it within their very own unique and individual frame of reference. And this means that whatever you thought your song was about, whatever you intended it to mean or say, is really irrelevant. Because every listener has the right to interpret it however they like.

This might seem odd at, at first, but it can actually be liberating. In a way, your listeners become collaborators. Their perception of your song has as much weight – if not more – than you, the songwriter.

I once got a letter (you know, hundreds of years ago, before email) in which an enthusiastic fan expounded on the hidden meanings in my song, 'Ariel'.

He was convinced that the lyrics were riddled with sexual innuendo. And considering the fact that the song climaxes with the line, *'We made love to bombs bursting in Aaaaaaariel.'* I was in no position to argue with him. However, he went on to explain that lyrics I had imagined to be completely innocent and benign, were, in fact, none-too-subtle, sexual references, suggesting that my lyric mentioning *onion rings* and a *pickle* meant something else entirely:

We went to Dairy Queen for something to eat.
She had some onion rings. She had a pickle.
She forgot to tell me that she didn't eat meat.

He continued to expound on how, in the following verse, a

reference to, *'fooling around with the vertical hold'*, was obviously an explicit reference to making-out:

> *I took her home with me. We watched some TV,*
> *Annette Funicello and some guy going steady.*
> *I started fooling around with the vertical hold.*
> *We got the munchies and I made some spaghetti.*

Truth is I used to have an old black & white TV set with lousy reception and in order to stabilize the picture you had to constantly re-adjust the vertical and horizontal hold. I was being quite literal. The suspect line was perfectly innocent. Or at least I had believed so at the time I wrote it.

Because, regardless of what my original intent might have been, he wasn't wrong. His interpretation of my lyrics was every bit as valid as my own.

And so I had no reason to disabuse him of his lengthy and risqué analysis.

> *"Songwriters write songs, but they really belong to the listener."* - Jimmy Buffett

I've grown accustomed to this curious phenomenon. It's just another amazing aspect of songwriting. Once freed, released into the wild, songs take on a life of their own. And like little kids, all you can do is hope they do well in the world.

NOTE: Oddly enough, some songs – even songs released into the wild - are never actually finished. Case in point: The wonderful songwriter, Christine Lavin, a genuine treasure of the contemporary, American folk scene (go see her in concert, she's amazing!), wrote a delightfully funny song, back in 1993 titled, 'What Was I Thinking?', which expressed hilarious incredulity at some of her own, and others', questionable life choices. She pokes fun at her dubious fashion picks and at receiving an ill-advised new hair-style…

What was he thinking?
I can't believe what I see
I look in the mirror
Art Garfunkel's looking back at me
What was he thinking?
Quick! Steal me a hat
I should look on the bright side
Unlike Art, at least mine will grow back.

The only problem is, every time another preposterous event occurs in Christine's life, she adds another hilarious verse to this never ending song. Year after year, audiences look forward to hearing the latest comical incarnation of 'What Was I Thinking', and I suspect there is a special category in the US Copyright Office for registering this song-that-has-no-end.

CO-WRITING AND SONG CIRCLES

Although I've only co-written songs on a very few occasions, the results were always successful and personally satisfying, and I would recommend it wholeheartedly. One doesn't have to look very far to realize that many of the greatest songs of all time were written by collaborators; songwriting teams, co-writers merging their talents to work creative alchemy in order to produce brilliant songs. Co-writing is a tried and true way to help generate new ideas, new perspectives, new approaches to writing a song and every songwriter should try it. In a place like Nashville – music city – co-writing is often seen as the rule rather than the exception.

But whether you write solo or as part of a pair, or trio, or more, one thing I would emphatically recommend is participation in a local song-circle, song-convention or song-festival. There is guaranteed to be a song-circle somewhere in your community, and if, by some odd quirk of fate, there's not, well then, start your own. In a typical song-circle, a group of songwriters will gather in a circle, with their instruments, and share their songs with each other, one by one, while offering each other useful feedback, positive criticism and support. A rich community spirit permeates the proceedings, and it's an invaluable opportunity for songwriters to meet and interact with their songwriting peers. It will make you a better songwriter.

I've always gotten a lot out of every song-circle I've ever attended, and regardless of their level of experience or professional credits or lack thereof, I continue to learn something new from every single songwriter I hear. So will you. Each individual voice and unique style of expression is a revelation to me. And I've learned something else from the song-circles I've attended, and that is, that some of the best songwriters in the world may never be heard on the radio or MTV or VH1 or any other mainstream music outlet; but you may very likely hear them in your own community, in your own town, in your own backyard. No shit!

> *"I'm from a little island off of Massachusetts, Nantucket. It's hard getting into the music business from there, but my parents took me to songwriting festivals because I would write and produce my own music."*
> - Meghan Trainor

THE POWER OF A SONG

According to the national newspaper, the Independent, *"'Lyrics' is one of the most top searched terms on Google... song lyrics are becoming the most effective medium for conveying social messages to young people, with more than a billion web searches each month seeking musical words of wisdom."*

And despite film producer, Samuel L Goldwyn's, maxim about never mixing entertainment with politics - *"If you want to send a message, call Western Union."* – no one doubts the important role songs have played, throughout history, in educating, galvanizing and comforting the political underclass of every era.

Songs have the power to teach, to inspire, to entertain, to soothe, to caution, to delight, to sadden, to amuse, to break hearts and mend them, to connect and unite, to illuminate and reveal, to remind us of things we've forgotten or never knew we knew, and to make us question our assumptions about ourselves and the world around us.

Songs have the ability to reach deep inside of us, into our psyches and our souls, in ways impossible to analyze or explain.

> *"I think music has the power to transform people, and in doing so, it has the power to transform situations - some large and some small."* - Joan Baez

I know I started out this book claiming that *it's the creation of the song itself, that's important,* and that if someone else happened to like it, well, that was great, but *not absolutely necessary.*

I'll admit now that, while I still believe that to be essentially true, songs *are meant to be heard*, to be shared and to be enjoyed by others.

I'll share this one last anecdote about songwriting and the power of a song.

Back in my early 20's, when I was enjoying the very first flush of commercial success as a recording artist, with a hit record soaring to the top of the charts, jetting off all over the world to do TV appearances on Dick Clark's 'American Band Stand' and Don Kirschner's 'Rock Concert' and 'Top of the Pops', a good friend from my neighborhood stopped me in Riverside Park.

Ronnie, was an elementary school teacher in Bedford Stuyvesant, a poor section of Brooklyn, where he spent his days looking after an overcrowded classroom filled with eager but disadvantaged kids. To give his students somewhere to go after class ended, Ron had started a boy scout troupe; an audacious move in a neighborhood where knives were typically used for things other than whittling sticks to roast marshmallows around a campfire. He had managed to secure a small amount of funding to take his troupe on their first Boy Scout camping trip and he excitedly announced that he was appointing me his assistant scout master. My dog, Barker, was appointed troupe patrol leader.

The next weekend, after, first, confiscating a dozen switchblades from our excited scouts, we piled into an old yellow school bus and headed off for the William H. Pouch Boy Scout Camp in Staten Island. To pass the time on the long bus ride out to the campgrounds, I made up a silly 'call and response' boot-camp, marching song, on the spot. The repeating chanted refrain went like this:

> *We are the Scouts!*
> *(We are the Scouts!)*
> *Of One Three Five!*
> *(Of One Three Five!)*
> *We're the hippest Scouts alive!*
> *(We're the hippest Scouts alive!)*

The many verses, which they sang at the top of their lungs (much to the chagrin of the bus driver), included...

> *We're so cool!*
> *We have no cares!*
> *We play poker with the bears!*
>
> *We are the Scouts...*
>
> *When we go swimmin'*
> *In the lake,*
> *We play tag with the water snakes!*
>
> *We are the Scouts...*
>
> *We're so fast,*
> *Would you believe,*
> *We get back before we leave!*
>
> *We are the Scouts...*
>
> *We look so good!*
> *We look so fine!*

We comb our hair with a porcupine!

We are the Scouts...

We arrived at the campgrounds and as we made our way through the woods to our camp site, I noticed with surprise that our ragtag scout troupe, most of whom had never stepped into a forest before, had suddenly turned from a ghetto-tough gang of city kids into a wide-eyed group of little boys, in awe at the sights and sounds and smells of the majestic forest all around them.

After setting up camp, our enthusiastic troupe made its way to the camp dining hall to join the rest of the scout troupes for assembly and a meal. But as soon as we filed into the large room and took our seats at a long dining table, the mood of our kids grew suddenly somber.

It only took me a few moments, and a quick glance around the room, to determine the cause. Every other scout troupe, all from affluent suburbs, was outfitted in spanking brand new uniforms, festooned with colorful badges and shiny pins and kerchiefs and sashes and caps. All except for us. Troupe #135, the kids from Bed Stye. We had barely scraped up enough funding to pay for the campgrounds and a rickety old school bus, and our kids came from families for whom food and rent money was a constant challenge, and fancy uniforms an inconceivable luxury.

The kids ate their meal in silence, until it was time to clear our table, and I stood up, said, 'listen up!', and started calling out our marching song. At once, their eyes lit up and they leapt to their feed singing with intense fervor. They marched from one end of the dining hall to the other, carrying their dirty food trays, and singing their hearts out, to the astonishment of everyone else in the room.

We are the Scouts!
(We are the Scouts!)
Of One Three Five!
(Of One Three Five!)
We're the hippest Scouts alive!
(We're the hippest Scouts alive!)

They emptied their trays and marched back across the room,

back to their table, singing all the way, their voices bouncing off the rafters,

> *We're so cool!*
> *We have no cares!*
> *We play poker with the bears!*

...weaving through benches packed with uniformed campers who, having recovered from their shock, were now listening intently and looking on in visible envy at our troupe of proud, joyful, city kids who, though they lacked fancy uniforms, had their very own Boy Scout Troup #135 marching song.

For the rest of the weekend, Boy Scout Troup #135 continued to sing their song everywhere they went, from one end of the camp to another. You could hear them marching and singing along the trails and around the lake and around the campfires before they finally hunkered down into their tents and sleeping bags, at the end of the day, and fell fast asleep.

I've had hit records all over the world and have gold records on my wall. I've written songs for TV and movies, virtual reality video games and national ad campaigns, had covers by top bands, won awards. I've written a lot of songs that I'm proud of.

But of all of the hundreds of songs I've written, over my entire music career, the one I'm most proud of is, 'We Are the Scouts of 135', the marching song of Boy Scout Troupe #135.

It's never been recorded. It's never been on the radio. It's never hit the charts or been awarded a gold record or a Grammy.

But one day, many years ago, at a campground in the middle of the woods in Staten Island, NY, that little scrap of a song turned a small group of embarrassed, dejected little kids into a proud, joyful, beaming troupe of boy scouts.

If pressed, I'd have to say it's the best song I ever wrote.

WRAPPING UP

I could say a lot more about songwriting – but I won't. I've tried to touch on what I consider to be the most important aspects of the job – and yes, it is a job, as well as a way of looking at the world - and, hopefully, at least some of it will prove useful in your own songwriting endeavors. Let me know how it goes!

In conclusion I'm going to leave you with a few quick and easy recipes for writing a song, derived from the previous chapters in this book. If any of them actually come in handy, great. But remember, there are many ways to bake a cat, I mean skin a cake. I mean... you know what I mean. The actual recipe should be tailored to the individual. Feel free to substitute ingredients as needed.

[WARNING: DON'T LEAVE YOUR CAKE OUT IN THE RAIN!]**[1]**

HOW TO WRITE A SONG IN 20 EASY STEPS

1. Sleep late
2. Eat a leisurely breakfast
3. Read the paper
4. Sit your ass down and choose your weapon (instrument or word processor, DAW (digital audio workstation or all-of-the-above)
5. Improvise
6. Go for a walk
7. Improvise
8. Watch some TV
9. Improvise
10. Once you stumble upon a music or lyric idea that you like, play with it a while, and start thinking about what direction you plan on taking it (idiom, harmonic vocabulary, tempo, key, persona, p.o.v., etc...) Then, make some choices.
11. Figure out what your song is about
12. Ask questions about your song's topic (do some research!)
13. Scribble (or type) a bunch of words, phrases and ideas that pertain to your song's topic.
14. Ask more questions about those words, phrases and ideas and then scribble down more words, phrases and ideas based on your own answers to those questions.
15. Write a whole bunch of couplets and stanzas using those words, phrases and ideas.

---

[1] With all due credit and respect to the great, Jimmy Webb.

16. Arrange those couplets and stanzas into some kind of lyrical/musical song structure (verse, chorus and/or bridge forms)
17. Conduct song triage. Prioritize what's absolutely necessary and start whittling down your verses and choruses by keeping the best stuff and getting rid of the rest. (and only if the best stuff actually serves the song; no matter how good it is, if it doesn't serve the song, cut it. You can always use it someplace else.).
18. See if you can find ways to further edit your best material to refine it ever more. (the stew's not done until you've added all the ingredients, and)
19. Keep tweaking and refining it until it's ready to take out of the oven – or wait, I forgot we were making a stew – until it's ready to take off of the stove and serve to guests.
20. Play your song. Then, repeat steps 1 through 20.

And for those of you with actual jobs, that are really pressed for time, here's the EVEN QUICKER super-fast, instant song recipe.

HOW TO WRITE A SONG IN 10 EASY STEPS

1. **Improvise.**
2. **Choose** a direction.
3. **Figure out** what your song is about.
4. **Ask** questions about your song's topic.
5. **Generate** ideas
6. Write **couplets**.
7. **Arrange** your couplets into a song structure.
8. Conduct song *triage.*
9. **Edit** and **tweak.**
10. **Pick up** the kids at day-care

And finally for folks who don't like being told what to do or how to do it – and know most of this stuff anyway - and really just need a little gentle nudging in the right direction…

HOW TO WRITE A SONG IN 2 EASY STEPS

1. Ignore everything I just said because the truth is – and I mean this – regardless of your inexperience, you know how to write your own song a whole lot better than I do, 'cause

after all I'm not you, and it's your song, and seriously, no shit - it's not that hard!

2. Sit down, start strumming or typing or humming, and write the fucking song.

Thanks for listening.

Happy songwriting!

Dean

DEAN FRIEDMAN

'Songwriter's Handbook' Playlist

The following url contains YouTube links for most of the songs mentioned in this book. You're encouraged to occasionally stop and listen as you read through the different sections of this book. Enjoy the music!

www.deanfriedman.com/songwriters-handbook-playlist.html

Pg 3	**Happy Birthday**	by Mildred & Patty Hill
Pg 9	**Norwegian Wood**	by John Lennon
	Fourth Time Around	by Bob Dylan
Pg 10	**Blackbird**	by Paul McCartney
	Company	by Dean Friedman and Stuffy Shmitt
	Bourrée in E minor	by J.S. Bach's
Pg 12	**Yesterday**	by Paul McCartney
Pg 14	**Ode to a Snail** (I Like You)	by Dean Friedman
Pg 16	**Hanging on the Telephone**	by Jack Lee
	Lay Lady Lay	by Bob Dylan
	The Shadow of Your Smile	by Johnny Mandel and Paul Francis Webster
	Traces	by Buddy Buie, J.R. Cobb and Emory Gordy, Jr.
	Every Picture Tells a Story	by Rod Stewart and Ronnie Wood
	Hob-Nobbin'	by Dean Friedman
Pg 17	**From a Distance**	by Julie Gold
Pg 18	**Doint, Doint, It's Just a Little Joint'**	by Dean Friedman
Pg 25	**You and Me, Cat**	by Dan Pelletier
Pg 29	**Born in the USA**	by Bruce Springsteen
	Maria	by Leonard Bernstein and Stephen Sondheim
	I Could Have Danced All Night	by Alan Jay Lerner and Frederick Loewe
	Till There Was You	by Meredith Willson
	If I Fell	by Lennon and McCartney
Pg 30	**Do You Want to Know a Secret**	by Lennon and McCartney
	Help!	by Lennon and McCartney
	Money for Nothing	by Mark Knofler
Pg 31	**Someone Like You**	by Adele and Dan Wilson
	Video Games	by Lana Del Rey and Justin Parker
	MacArthur Park	by Jimmy Webb
Pg 32	**Wouldn't it be Nice**	by Brian Wilson, Tony Asher and Mike Love
	America	by Paul Simon
	And I Love Her	by Lennon & McCartney
	I Should Have Known Better	by Lennon & McCartney

DEAN FRIEDMAN

....

ABOUT THE AUTHOR

Dean Friedman wrote his first song at the age of nine, titled, 'I'd Love to Take a Swim With You in the Summertime'. Since then, he's enjoyed hit records around the world, including, 'Ariel', 'Lucky Stars', 'Lydia', 'Woman of Mine', "Well, Well," Said the Rocking Chair' and 'McDonald's Girl', a track covered by Barenaked Ladies, and featured in a national TV/Radio campaign by a certain fast-food hamburger chain. He has composed and produced soundtracks for TV and Film, including 'Boon', 'Eerie Indiana', 'Total Panic', 'Nick Arcade' and 'I Bought a Vampire Motorcycle', and has won awards for his music videos, 'I Miss Monica' and 'A Terrible Pickle'. His song, 'Doint, Doint, It's Just a Little Joint', won Best Comedy Song at the American Marijuana Music Awards. Friedman is the creator of 'Eat-a-Bug', the world's first VR game for Nickelodeon TV and developed the VR games for Nickelodeon's classic VR game show, Nick Arcade. His VR game environments and Music Atriums - musical playgrounds for kids – are featured at leading children's museums and theme parks. Friedman is the author of, 'Synthesizer Basics', and producer/host of the popular, New York School of Synthesis 'Intro to Synthesis' video series, featured on YouTube. It's been rumored that Friedman is the anonymous author of 'A Musician's Guide to Surviving the Great Recession' by A. Musician, but we can neither confirm nor deny such a rumor. Dean continues to write, record and tour, and conducts Songwriting Workshops and Masterclasses at universities around the world.

If you'd to learn more about Dean's music and Songwriting Workshops and Skype Seminars, simply send an email to:

dean@deanfriedman.com

or visit Dean's website at

www.DeanFriedman.com